THE
MAKING OF AMERICA
SERIES

TROY

A COLLAR CITY HISTORY

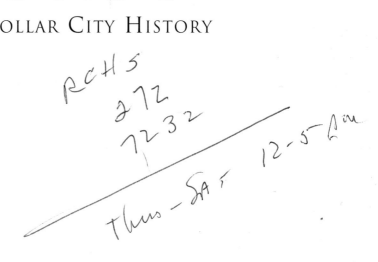

The elegant interior of Troy's Union Station is pictured here around 1904. It was torn down for a parking lot but now is the site of the Raddock Building.

THE
MAKING OF AMERICA
SERIES

TROY
A COLLAR CITY HISTORY

DON RITTNER

ARCADIA
PUBLISHING

First published 2002
Reprinted 2006

Published by Arcadia Publishing
Charleston SC, Chicago IL, Portsmouth NH, San Francisco CA

Library of Congress control number: 2002100851

For all general information contact Arcadia Publishing at:
Telephone 843-853-2070
Fax 843-853-0044
E-Mail sales@arcadiapublishing.com
For customer service and orders:
Toll-Free 1-888-313-2665

Visit us on the Internet at www.arcadiapublishing.com

To Louis F. Ismay

a mentor and friend,

an inspiration to us all.

CONTENTS

Acknowledgments

Many people have helped in the preparation of this book, although any errors in interpretation are my own. I thank the following for their contributions: Dr. Ed Landing, New York State Paleontologist, and his colleagues Linda Van Aller Hernick and Sharon Mannolini; Greta Wagle, Capital District Preservation Task Force; Dr. P. Thomas Carroll, Executive Director, Hudson Mohawk Industrial Gateway; Tom and Ray Clement, Clement Frame Shop at 201 Broadway, for the use of several images; Greg DeJulio and Frank Merola, Rensselaer County Clerk's Office; Albany historian John Wolcott; Lansingburgh historian Warren Broderick; Roger Wood; Bob Falk; Steven Comer, representative, Stockbridge-Munsee Band of Mohican Indians; historian Shirley W. Dunn; John Nehrich and Gerritt Bruins, Rensselaer Railroad Heritage Center collection; NOAA Photo Library, NOAA Central Library; the family of Captain William M. Scaife, C&GS; Commander John Bortniak, NOAA Corps; Library of Congress, Prints and Photographs Division; Jim Macy; Trudy Hall, Susan H. Geary, and Barbara Wiley from Emma Willard School; Brown University Library Collection; David R. Smith; U.S.Naval Historical Center; Nancy, Chris, Kevin, and Jack Rittner; Rensselaer Polytechnic Institute (RPI) Archives; Jim Shaughnessy, transportation historian and photographer; Smithsonian Institution; John E. Swantek, Director, Watervliet Arsenal Museum; Marjory Roddy and St. Paul's Episcopal Church; my editor, Mark Berry, for his patience; and for those that are inadvertently left out, my apologies.

INTRODUCTION

Trying to write the history of Troy, New York, in 160 pages is equivalent to trying to fit a gallon of water in a thimble. It's impossible. Let me apologize that this book presents only a snapshot of the history of a city that has made history as much its byproduct as iron or collars.

Troy is not a large city physically. It only encompasses a few square miles of Rensselaer County, some 150 miles north of New York City. The city is situated on a flood plain of the Hudson River, and draped along the Rensselaer escarpment to the east. Albany, the state capital, is a neighbor a few miles south. Other communities adjacent to Troy include Watervliet, Cohoes, Green Island, and Waterford, much of this considered at one time part of "Greater Troy."

During the nineteenth century, Troy was an industrial giant, and yet the city was physically smaller than today, compacted into a few streets along the riverfront, and barely reaching past Fifth Avenue, hugging the base of Mount Ida to the east and the stream beds of the Wyantskill and Poestenkill. Specialized industries developed in various parts of the city. Iron and steel settled in the south end. Collars and cuffs migrated to north central and the riverfront. Brush making congregated in the north, and commercial and retail concentrated in the downtown business area between Chatham Square and Ferry Streets.

Neighborhoods developed around the social and cultural traditions of the immigrant workforce. There were defined neighborhoods of Irish, Italians, Jews, Scots, African Americans, and others, and names like Brownsville, Scottsville, or Batestown reflected those ethnic concentrations. To this day, one can often hear the phrase "South Troy against the World," spoken like a true mantra and displaying a strong identification with where one grew up in Troy. Trojans are proud to be Trojans.

One can find a Trojan contribution in almost any major American event over the last 200 years. To understand Troy's history is to admire "American" history. The entrepreneurial output of Troy's nineteenth-century citizenry represents all that can be realized when the synergy of freedom and vision are left unhampered.

Troy is a city where its citizens seem to have had their hands in everything. Only Pittsburgh, Pennsylvania, rivaled it as an iron center during the nineteenth century. Troy dominated the collar and cuff market, an industry it created. There are probably more bells ringing around the world with the Troy name on it than any other manufacturer.

Trojans contributed heavily in all wars, not only in human sacrifice, but in making major contributions to armament designs, including financing and rolling the plates for the famous ironclad *Monitor* during the Civil War. Military leaders such as John Wool and Joseph B. Carr were noted decorated soldiers. Troy was a player in the Underground Railroad and promoted the abolition of slavery, even staging the first American production of the play *Uncle Tom's Cabin* for 150 consecutive nights. In fact, there were no slaves in Troy for 30 years before the Civil War.

Troy is the home of the real "Uncle Sam" Wilson, who provided meat to the troops during the War of 1812. He also made bricks. Troy was the birthplace of American geology, started by Amos Eaton as early as 1818. The first female college, Emma Willard's Troy Female Seminary, began here in 1821 and proved that women could learn the same subjects as men. The first college devoted to science, Amos Eaton's Rensselaer School (now Rensselaer Polytechnic Institute, or RPI), began only three years later. Even in entertainment, Troy can boast of being the birthplace and home of Maureen Stapleton, contemporary star of stage, screen, and television, who was born on First Street. For a small city, Troy was a powerhouse of influence around the world.

In this book I have tried to paint a picture of a city, its citizens, and the entrepreneurial spirit that is hard to duplicate elsewhere. Within the limitations of this volume, I can only focus on a few choice industries, but it should be noted here that many industries flourished in this city. It wasn't simply iron and collars that made Troy great, but I can barely touch on social and cultural issues in this short treatment. When one surveys the inventive output of Troy, a pattern clearly emerges. If a Trojan saw a need, he, or she, quickly created the product to satisfy it. There seems to have been an understanding that anything and everything was possible when one lived in Troy.

However, nothing survives forever, and Troy, like most industrial cities of the Northeast, has struggled over the last 30 years as manufacturers and laborers migrated out of the region. Yet, Troy is undergoing an economic revival and a heritage renaissance and success is pretty much a guarantee. The city may never be a manufacturing giant again, but the entrepreneurial spirit still exists in Troy and will allow it to develop and lead in other industries, be it education, high tech, or heritage tourism. After all, if history has proven anything, it has shown that one cannot keep Troy down for very long.

This book only provides a small window into a rich history, but I hope it will stimulate readers to look further. At the end of this volume readers will find a list of books that can help complete this story.

—Don Rittner
January 2002

1. FIRE, ICE, AND WATER
THE ORIGINS OF TROY

The landscape of Troy and its environs did not always look the way it does now. The underlying geology was created over millions of years by physical processes that are still in action, but the observable landscape was sculpted only about 20,000 years ago during the terminal stages of the last ice age. However, the primary geological activity responsible for the characteristic features of Troy's landscape took place far longer ago.

Although it seems the ground one walks on is pretty solid, the truth is that it is moving. Slowly perhaps, but the ground is definitely moving you and everything around you. For example, the distance between North America (including the United States and Troy) and Western Europe increases about 2 inches a year.

The earth's surface and upper layers, to a depth of about 90 miles, are divided into about 40 slowly moving, scale-like units called "plates." Some plates are so large that they have a continent or two as their highest points (North and South America and the east Atlantic Ocean are all on one plate). These plates float like giant icebergs on deeper and much denser rock that churns with a motion similar to that of boiling water. This churning motion is called a "convection current." Convection currents rise where they are hot and descend where they are cold.

Here's how plate movement involves modern North America. A pair of convection cells are now rising under the central Atlantic. As they rise, they move east and west and away from each other. This movement works to widen the Atlantic, and molten rock (seen in modern Iceland) rises to fill the cracks. With further movement to the east and west, both western North and South America and the eastern margin of Asia are being pushed over the Pacific Ocean and are slowly narrowing the Pacific. A great series of volcanoes called the "Rim of Fire" has developed at all locations where the Pacific is being overridden by the Americas and Eurasian plates.

What is the relevance to Troy? All of these dynamic processes—called plate tectonics— such as the continuing movement of the ocean floors with spreading from the center, sinking at the edges, the collision of continents, and uplift of mountains as plates collide, acted in the geologic past and can be reconstructed from rocks like those at Troy.

Our modern evidence of plate tectonics is shown by precision satellite determinations of the movement of the earth's surface and by scientific study of earthquake records from

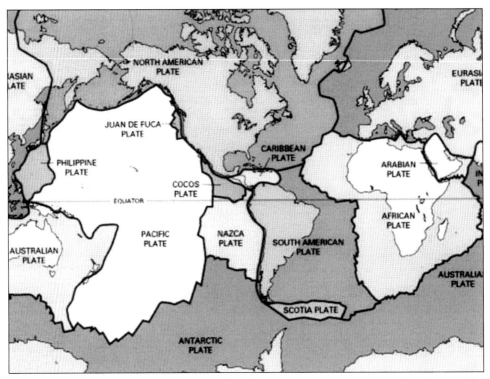

The Earth is made up of many "plates" that float above the molten core of the planet. The North American plate abuts several other larger and smaller plates.

seismographs. We experience plate tectonics during earthquakes or volcanic eruptions, and we now understand that the source of heat driving these convection currents is a byproduct of radioactive decay deep in the earth's mantle.

Over the last 500 million years, the bedrock of our region developed as a result of a complex history that included deposition of sands, muds, and limy deposits in an ocean that no longer exists, collision with a volcanic island chain now fossilized in central New England that led to intense metamorphism and folding, and lastly, a blanketing and carving by the actions of the last glacial advance.

Much of our region is underlain by surface rocks dominated by shale, siltstone, and sandstone. At great depths under Troy, but at the surface in Glen Falls and Saratoga, tropical limestones and dolostone, oddly, so it would seem, of the same age as the surface rocks are found. Finally, the deep basement of Troy, about 10,000 feet down, is composed of billion-year-old rocks identical to the Adirondacks and Hudson Highlands. In general, valleys like that occupied by the Hudson River are underlain by soft and easily eroded rocks.

The highlands immediately east of the Hudson and underlying Poestenkill gorge, RPI, and Oakwood Cemetery are composed of much harder rock, and this contrast gives the area a rolling and mountainous, picturesque quality. In general, Route 4 north of North Troy follows a line that separates the lowlands from the more resistant Taconic Hills. The higher Taconic Mountains to the east of Troy on the state line are largely metamorphosed shale and sandstone.

It is difficult to give a "nutshell summary" of the geologic history of Troy—but it is also this complexity that led to the birth of North American geology and paleontology in the early 1800s as a result of the study of rocks in the New York Capital region. Indeed, the first understanding that mountain belts were not permanent features on the earth that arose at Creation or during a Biblical flood originated in the 1860s with the study of the belt of rocks from Troy to Poughkeepsie. This work by New York State paleontologist James Hall was then applied by European geologists to help explain the origin of the Alps.

Let us try this "nutshell summary" of Troy-area geology that involves several openings and closings of oceans at the margins of North America.

The story begins about one billion years ago when ancestral North America underwent a truly massive collision with what is today part of Northern Europe. Called the Grenville mountain-building event, a range of mountains was uplifted as high as the modern Himalayas that extended from Greenland along the eastern margin of North America and down to central Mexico. The modern Adirondacks, Green Mountains, and Berkshires east of Troy, Hudson Highlands, and Blue Ridge are all uplifted parts of this ancient basement that was once almost melted at a depth of 25 miles underground. With the Grenville mountain building, all modern continents were clustered together in a supercontinent geologists call Rodinia. However, supercontinents never last. They form over an interval of 300 million years and then break apart into many continents, only to form again. About 600 million years ago, Rodinia began to break apart. One of these major breaks ran east of Troy about along the modern Connecticut River Valley. Troy lay not too far from the edge of a widening ocean, called Iapetus by geologists, that formed the east side of Laurentia, or "Proto-North America."

Early in the Cambrian geological period, about 520 million years ago, shallow sea water at the edge of Iapetus covered eastern Laurentia and the Troy area. These tropical seas laid down sandstones, like those at Ausable Chasm on the east side of the Adirondacks, and thick deposits of very fossil-rich limestones, similar to those in the modern Caribbean. This was all to be expected, as plate tectonics had moved east Laurentia to about 35 degrees south latitude. At a great distance offshore, perhaps 60 to 75 miles east, deep-water muds and sands were laid down. These muds and sands in central Massachusetts are vital to the Troy story, since they now make up much of the Troy region. At times, storms or collapses, perhaps brought about by earthquakes, caused the shallow limestone shelf to collapse and transport fossils far east into deep water.

A famous example of this sort of event is preserved in the rocks of Beman Park in Troy. In the 1870s, S.W. Ford, a Troy resident and amateur paleontologist, found fossils called archaeocyathans in limestone boulders in Beman Park. These are extinct, reef-building sponges with limy skeletons. Not only were these the first archaeocyathans found in North America and for some time the oldest fossils found in the United States, but they helped James Hall devise his theory of mountain building.

Briefly summarized, Ford's discovery showed that the rocks on the ridges and in Poestenkill gorge in Troy were far older than the rocks at lower elevations along the Hudson River. As younger rocks should overlie older rocks (geologists call this the principal of "superposition"), great earth movements including faults involved in mountain building had to be invoked.

The division of eastern North America into shallow tropical seas covering the continent and deep-water sands and muds farther offshore persisted for about 120 million years. It ended with the onset of the first mountain-building episode of the northern Appalachians—the Taconic mountain-building episode that created most of the bedrock features of the area. This Taconic orogeny (*i.e.*, mountain-building interval) about 450 million years ago resulted from plate tectonic activity that led to the collision of a volcanic island arc—similar to modern Japan—with eastern Laurentia.

During this volcanic arc–continent collision, the sands and muds deposited in central Massachusetts were pushed west into New York and across the tropical limestone shelf rocks. Once lying flat, the rock layers of both the shelf and the offshore sequence were folded, pushed up, and broken by faults. The volcanic island arc and bulldozed sediments from central Massachusetts were uplifted as a low mountain range (perhaps 5,000 to 6,000 feet high) and were eroded by tropical rains. The eroded sediments eventually spread across Laurentia as far as modern Minnesota, and obviously blanketed the Troy area. These Middle Ordovician age (*c.* 450 million years ago) muds are now the soft rocks of the Hudson River Valley and are best seen on the west side of the river in Watervliet and Menands.

The relentless pressure caused by the pushing of the east margin of Laurentia under the island arc at what is called a subduction zone eventually pushed the sands and muds from central Massachusetts across the Troy region and at least as far west as Saratoga Lake. Cambrian rocks were forced across the Middle Ordovician muds and sands of the Hudson River Valley. The fault surface under the Taconic overthrust is known as the "Emmons line"—named for Ebenezer Emmons, head of the geology department at RPI in the early 1800s, who recognized that some sort of disturbance separated overlying older from underlying younger rocks. Emmons Line is marked by giant blocks of rock ripped from the overthrust and from underlying Laurentia. Some of these blocks are up to 6 miles long. Bald Mountain north of Troy is really a giant block of Lower Ordovician limestone at the base of the Taconic thrust. Similarly, Stark's Knob just north of Schuylerville is a block of Middle Ordovician volcanic rock (a pillow basalt) that erupted on the sea floor on the Laurentian side of the collision.

Taconic mountain building was followed by 430 million years of geologic history that have left little record in the immediate Troy area. The Silurian and early part of the Devonian periods (430–410 million years ago) were not marked by important mountain-building activity in the eastern United States. Tropical seas again covered the region and are recorded by the limestones of the Helderberg Mountains on the skyline southwest of Albany. These rocks once covered Troy, but are now eroded away.

The record of later mountain-building events in the Appalachians are not distinguishable in the Troy area. The Iapetus Ocean closed in the Middle and Late Devonian with the collision of a small continent called Avalon and most of the eastern United States and Canada. This collision is called the Acadian Orogeny. Avalon, which was probably about the size of New Zealand, is now incorporated as coastal New England and Maritime Canada. By some interpretations, one result of the collision of Avalon was the uplift of the

Green Mountains east of Troy. Sands and muds eroded from the Acadian belt now make up the high peaks of the Catskill Mountains.

The last mountain-building event in the northern Appalachians featured the collision of west Africa with the eastern United States and adjacent Canada. Effects of this major collision in the Carboniferous period, or Coal Age, 350 to 286 million years ago, can be reconstructed in Maritime Canada and from New York City south, but its effects are not seen in the Troy area. With this last mountain-building interval, all the continents were again clustered into a supercontinent; this time called Gondwana.

The break-up of Gondwana is reflected in Troy's geography. Gondwana split apart along the modern east coast of the United States and Maritime Canada. A major fault line ran off at an angle of about 60 degrees from the New York Bight and up the trend of the modern Hudson River. Red sands and muds were laid down along the trend of this fault in Staten Island and the southern Hudson River Valley. Later on, the Hudson River would develop along the trend of these soft rocks and would erode its valley north past Troy along the trend of the Middle Ordovician mudrocks of the Troy lowlands.

The last stage of the geologic evolution of Troy took place at the end of the last glacial episode. There were several ice advances that covered our world during the Pleistocene Epoch, which began some 20 million years ago. Evidence of earlier ice advances were

The Emmons line, where older Cambrian rocks have been thrust on top of younger Ordovician rocks, is clearly visible in the Mount Ida Falls area.

erased from the record by advances and retreats of those following. In Troy, there is plenty to look at, all of it left from the last ice age, the Wisconsin.

During the Wisconsin advance, the ice margin attained its maximum reach in New York State about 21,750 years ago, giving the state the appearance of present-day Antarctica. It left as a reminder of its most southern reach the area we call Long Island today. As the ice sheet, called the Laurentide (originating in Canada's Laurentian Mountains), moved south, its sandpaper effect scraped away soil and sediments, gouged river valleys, deposited materials, changed drainage systems, and generally altered the face of any area it encountered. As it began to retreat, only finally leaving the state some 10,000 years ago, it blanketed the area with more materials and landforms shaped by its actions, created lakes, and changed the course of rivers and streams.

After the ice sheet created Long Island by depositing huge amounts of terminal moraine, the climate began to warm and the ice sheet started its northern retreat over 20,000 years ago. The meltwater from the ice sheet released large volumes of water (enough worldwide to raise the ocean level 328 feet).

The ice sheet became stationary for a few thousand years as deposits (a terminal moraine) blocked the continued southern flow of meltwater, miles south of the Capital District region in the Hudson Highlands. The result was a slowly growing lake, called Glacial Lake Albany, which eventually filled most of the Hudson Valley and lasted

The Laurentide ice sheet, which extended down the Hudson River valley to the Atlantic, probably looked much like this modern glacier.

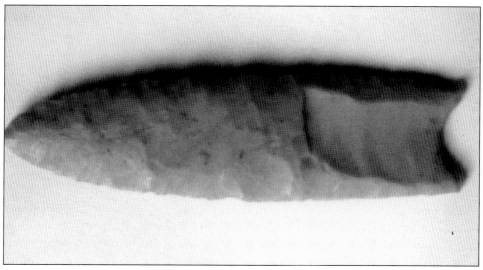

Clovis points, like this one from the Hudson Valley, were used by early Native Americans to kill large animals like the Cohoes mastodont.

between 20,000 and 13,000 years ago. Blockage of the lower Hudson River Valley meant that the outlet of Glacial Lake Albany was through the modern Wallkill River through New Jersey. This lake grew as wide as 31 miles and was 199 miles long, extending from the New York City area to Glens Falls. In the Albany area, it was almost 400 feet deep. Glacial Lake Albany at its highest elevation covered all of what is now the city of Troy, but the lake drained rather quickly, geologically speaking, in a series of gulps.

While Glacial Lake Albany existed in the Capital District region, streams from higher areas emptied into the lake forming submerged deltas and other lake deposits. The most important source of water from Glacial Lake Albany came from the Mohawk River—but this was a Mohawk River that served as the outlet of the Great Lakes and conduit of meltwater from the melting southern margins of ice sheets as far west as Chicago. The Mohawk not only rapidly filled Glacial Lake Albany with muds, but also supplied the sands that were blown by winds to form the sand dunes now known as the Pine Barrens (the Pine Bush) between Albany and Schenectady.

Other remnants of the glacial ice reveal features such as glacial till (hills called drumlins) and flat ground moraine, ice contact and outwash deposits (including the conical hills called kames), and eskers.

As you enjoy Troy's environs either by foot or vehicle, you are traversing the remnants of this fascinating geology. As you walk around downtown and work your way up to Fifth Avenue, you are walking on recent alluvium deposits left from the modern Hudson River, only a few thousands years old. However, go up to the "East Side" to Burdett Avenue and you are on clays and silts laid down by Glacial Lake Albany. The top of Mount Ida (Prospect Park) is lake-formed thin sands and pebbles draped on top of the Lake Albany clay beneath. Just east of Troy High School and running north to Frear Park are the thin gravel and clays that make up the beach of Lake Albany at the 330 foot level.

The Cohoes Falls between Troy and Cohoes was one of the ancient wonders of the New World and a popular tourist spot during the seventeenth and eighteenth centuries.

That's right—beachfront property if you live on either side of Sunset Terrace north to Pointview Drive.

Past the beach and into Sycaway are ice contact outwash gravel and esker deltas. From Emma Willard School west to and past Burden's Pond lies a sand delta formed when the Poestenkill and Wyantskill emptied into Glacial Lake Albany. Emma Willard School itself sits on ice contact outwash gravel and sands. There's glacial till just north and south of School 18. You can even view earlier Cambrian and Ordovician geology by looking at rock outcrops on Sage Avenue at RPI, or the northern flank of Mount Ida (Prospect Park) along Congress Street.

In the Poestenkill ravine itself, you can view the famous Emmons Line, a fault thrust where younger Ordovician rocks are lying under older Cambrian rocks (it should be the other way around). You can also view more recent ice contact formations there such as kames, kame terraces, and outwash gravel.

During the end of the ice age, the climate in our region was similar to modern subarctic areas—tundra-like, barren, and cold. Over the last several thousand years, the climate changed, passing through stages from tundra to spruce-fir forests, to forests of pine, and finally emerging into today's temperate zone of mixed deciduous forest.

However, during the Pleistocene Era (2,000,000 to 10,000 years ago) in our region, the environment was the home of mammoth and mastodonts, giant ground sloths, musk ox, seal, caribou, moose, bison, elk, horse, giant beaver, moose-elk, wild pigs (peccary), California condor, and others. Fossils of all have been recovered. Directly across the

Discovered in 1866 near Troy, the remains of the Cohoes mastodont are on display in the New York State Museum in Albany

Hudson River in nearby Cohoes, a mastodont was uncovered in 1866 when workers began excavating for the Cohoes Textile Mill No. 3 (at one time the largest textile mill in the country). A recent carbon 14 date revealed that the Cohoes mastodont died only 11,070 years ago.

It is believed that the first Native Americans reached the Troy area by following migrating herds of mammoth, caribou, and bison. In nearby Colonie, a Clovis point, a characteristic projectile point of early man, was found in the twentieth century. In fact, fluted points have been found in Albany, Schenectady, and Saratoga Counties, although none in Rensselaer County at the present time. There have been 297 fluted points found in all of New York State to date.

Whether these early residents of New York gave rise to the Native American groups encountered by the first European settlers is still much debated by archaeologists. But one thing is certain. The area of Troy was indeed populated by Native Americans when the Dutch settled here in the seventeenth century.

In summary, the Troy region shows evidence of ancient geological processes that are all around us and it is no wonder that the birth of American geology happened right here in Troy in the early nineteenth century.

2. Welcome to Mohican Land

History books claim that "the River of the Steep Hills" was discovered by Giovanni da Verrazzano in 1524, and explored by Hendrick Hudson in 1609, who called it the "River of Mountains." The mighty 315-mile-long Hudson River has had many names: the North River, Manhattes, Mauritius, Rio de Montaigne, Rio San Antonio, and "Muh-he-kun-ne-tuk" (where the waters were never still). In fact, the Hudson is not technically a river for half its length, but rather a fjord, or estuary, of the Atlantic Ocean.

This history, which is still promoted in some textbooks, is a bit arrogant as well as simply wrong considering both Verrazzano and Hudson encountered a diversity of native people during their explorations. They hadn't "discovered" anything, but merely stumbled on a region that was well settled by native people for probably thousands of years. Those native people greeting Hudson were indigenous people, the Algonquian-speaking "Muh-he ka-ne-ok," or Mahicans, today called the Mohicans.

Moreover, when you read the diaries and accounts of these voyages by Hudson or members of his crew, the reaction of the natives to the "newcomers" was not one of fear. Rather, they were eager to greet them and ready to trade for food and materials.

At the time Hudson reached our area, Troy was a forested river plain of red spruce, elm, pine, oak, maple, and birch trees with several fresh streams—the Piscawenkill, Meadow Creek, Poestenkill, and Wyantskill—all filled with fish, flowing down from the hills on the east draining into the Hudson River. Hudson's men saw fields growing corn, beans, and squash, while white-tailed deer, bear, moose, beaver, otter, bobcat, mink, wild turkey, and other animals abundantly filled the forests. They were equally impressed with the vast forests that covered the region. Writing in his journals, Hudson found, "The river is full of fish. . . . The land is the finest for cultivation that I ever in my life set foot upon."

The Mohicans already had named their homeland; they didn't need new ones from the Dutch or anyone else. "Paanpack" was the name applied to Troy along with "Gastanek" (Albany), "Nehanenesick" (Green Island), "Quahemesicos" (Van Schaick Island), "Mathahenaack" (Half Moon), and "Nachawinasick" (Cohoes).

The natives lived in small villages and towns stretched along the river banks and on higher ground. These villages were made up of circular wigwams composed of bent saplings covered with bark or reed mats, rectangular barrel-roofed houses, or long houses with roofs of elm bark, where the smoke of several fires could escape through holes every 20 feet or so.

Two palisaded villages bordered the north and south ends of the original Troy area: Monemius, or Moenemine's Castle, on Peeble's Island in the north across from present-day Lansingburgh, and Unawatt's Castle at the mouth of the Piscawenkill (though most histories attribute it to a location on the Poestenkill). Unawatt's village may have existed near present-day Hoosick Street, as a village was noted when one of the earliest Dutch settlers built his house a few feet south of it. Another village site may have existed on the east side of the river at Lansingburgh, across from Moenemine's. In this same region, a well-established flint mine and sacred burial grounds existed just to the north and south of the present Waterford Bridge. Native burials have been found on both sides of the Hudson. In essence, the Troy region was well settled by the time the Dutch arrived and had a rich human history already established.

How long the Mohicans and their ancestors lived in Troy is speculation at present and awaits discovery in the future by archaeologists. However, we do know that the area was occupied by indigenous people soon after Lake Albany left the area.

The Dutch began trading with the Mohicans, and later with the Mohawks to the west, soon after finding their way up the Hudson River. Hudson, for the most part, enjoyed his contact and trade, which included oysters, tobacco, currants, and many species of

This early engraving shows Henry Hudson approaching and greeting Native Americans (probably Mohicans) on his voyage upriver.

19

fish, including "young salmon and sturgeons." After Hudson reached the area, others such as Adrian Block and Henderick Christianson began regular yearly trading trips. The Mohicans looked forward to these visits and developed a mutual covenant of friendship and protection.

The first European settlement, temporarily at least, was Fort Nassau, built, with permission from the Mohicans, on an island just south of the Normanskill near present Albany. Mohicans gladly loaned the Dutch a plot of land on which to build the settlement that was to become Albany, just a few miles downriver from present-day Troy. Maps and written accounts leave no doubt that this was Mohican territory on both sides of the Hudson.

When the Dutch and later the English settled permanently on Mohican lands, visitors to the region often wrote about the beauty of the river, its contents, and shores. Two Dutch missionaries remarked, in 1679, "The North river abounds with fish of all kinds, throughout from the sea to the falls." When David Pieterzoon de Vries bought Staten Island in 1639, he visited the Albany region and found white and blue grapevines along the river, as well as swans, geese, pigeons, teal, and wild geese. The numerous islands in the river "were covered with chestnuts, plum, hazel nut, and large walnuts." In 1651, one Dutchman writing to another remarked about the abundance of cod and sturgeon in the river: "The sturgeon above all is in your rivers in such abundance and can be taken in such vast quantities that the Caviar could as well be manufactured there as muscovy." Sturgeon congregated at the base of the Cohoes Falls to propagate and were quite a sight to see, according to witnesses.

Sturgeon certainly was abundant in the Hudson. At one time, nearby Albany was called Sturgeonville and sturgeon was called "Albany Beef." Albany's citizens were called "Sturgeonites from Sturgeondom." Sturgeons ranged from 4 to 8 feet long and weighed from 100 to 450 pounds—one weighed in at 486 pounds. April to September was the harvest season, and about 20 per day were caught, often totalling about 2,500 per season; 100 barrels of oil were also extracted and used for lighting and medicinal purposes.

Adrian van der Donk, in 1654, called the river "seer visryck," Dutch for "very fish rich." He also wrote, perhaps prophetically, that his "attention was arrested by the Hudson, in which a painter could find rare and beautiful subjects for his brush." His keen observation came true. The Hudson River School of Painting appeared 200 years later.

In 1750, Peter Kalm wrote, "Sturgeons abound in the Hudson River. We saw them all day long leaping high up into the air, especially in the evening." He went on to say, "where the tide stops at the Hudson there being only a small and shallows streams above it. At that place they catch a good many kinds of fish in the river." Kalm continued with his natural history assessment, remarking on the various trees and wild grape vines "on the rising shores of the river, where some asparagus grew wild."

Herring, shad, bass, salmon, and other fish were also found in abundance. In 1804, one net yielded 40,000 shad in a single day. Fish was certainly an important part of the early diet among those who lived along the Hudson.

However, it was the beaver trade that proved to be a mixed blessing for the native population. For years, the Mohicans carried on trade with beaver pelts and traded for knives, clothes, and other implements. Today, we know the Mohican people inhabited

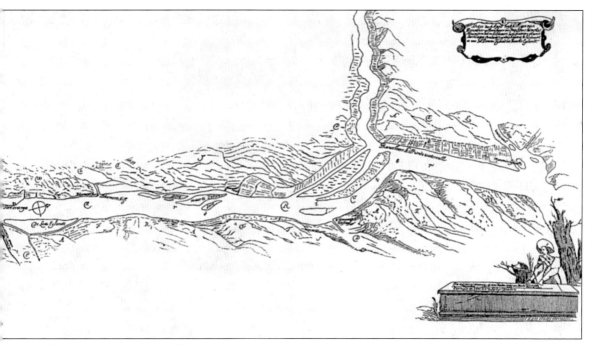

Three Mohican native villages occupied the Troy area when the Dutch first settled, as seen in this 1631 map.

the Hudson River Valley from the Catskill Mountains north to the southern end of Lake Champlain, west to the Schoharie River region extending east to the Berkshire Mountains in western Massachusetts, and from northwest Connecticut north to the Green Mountains in southern Vermont.

It was the Mohicans that allowed the Dutch a plot of land on which to create early Albany (Fort Nassau and Fort Orange), and looked upon themselves as protectors of the Dutch who lived among them. Yet, it was the competition from the Mohican's nearby enemy, the Mohawks to the west, and the land deals between the Dutch and Mohicans that proved detrimental to the long-term survival of the Mohican Nation. Their fate was sealed when they lost two wars with the Mohawks in 1625–1628 and 1660–1666. Many of them left the area to settle in Schaghitcoke on the Hoosick River, just north of Troy, eventually moving to Stockbridge, Massachusetts, and beyond. Their disappearance from the area was later immortalized, though inaccurately, in James Fenimore Cooper's book *The Last of the Mohicans*.

Only in recent years have we started to gain an understanding of the culture of the Mohicans who lived in our area, mostly through the research and publications of Shirley W. Dunn. Dunn's two books, *The Mohicans and Their Land: 1609–1730* and *The Mohican World: 1680–1750* (Purple Mountain Press, 1994 and 2000), trace much of the land transfer, via deeds, and the relationships between the early Dutch and Mohicans in the Hudson Valley and beyond. A review of the many deeds described in her books, as well as data from other researchers, gives us the following picture.

21

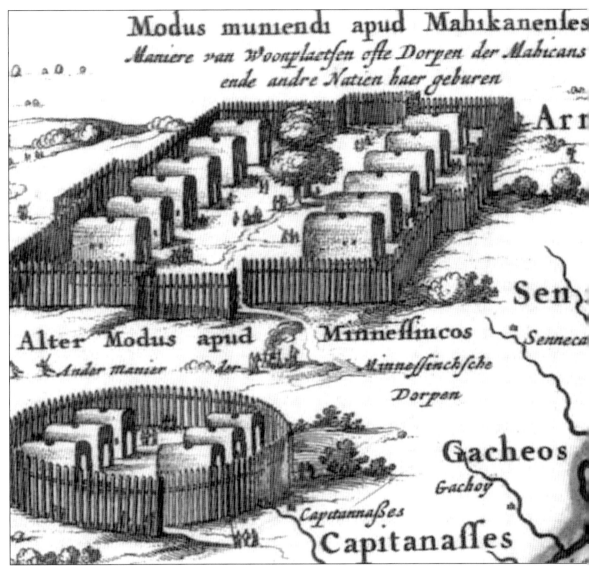

Mohicans lived in fortified villages during times of war with other nations, particularly the Mohawks to the west. This drawing is from an early seventeenth-century map.

When the Europeans arrived, and all during their contact, the Mohicans lived in small towns or villages in three divisions—the Mohican, Catskills, and Housatonic groups. Their central seat was in the Hudson Valley near Albany, or the general Albany area, and was called "Pempotowwuthut, Muhhhecanneuw," the "fireplace of the Muhheakunnuk nation." There may have been upwards of 8,000 people living in the region. Villages were protected by stockades during times of war.

While individual Mohicans controlled territories, they didn't always live in that territory. However, stream and river flats were highly prized areas for farming maize (corn), beans, and squash. Villages were spread throughout the territory not far from fertile flats, and in Rensselaer County, there were villages at Schodack, North Greenbush, Nassau, and the cities of Rensselaer and Troy's south end, downtown, and perhaps North Troy.

The Mohicans belonged to three clans: Wolf, Turtle, and Turkey. Historian Dunn has found all three represented in deed transactions with the Dutch. However, there appear to have been other clans or subclans represented by other animals and symbols, such as deer, snakes, eels (the Hudson abounds in them), and birds, as well as astronomical symbols. These symbols, however, may have had other significance now lost.

While clans were important, a single chief sachem was the head. For example, Aepjen was a Mohican chief sachem for about 20 years and bore witness to many deed signings. Both men and women could be sachems (chiefs) and are recorded on various local deeds as such.

There are more than 75 individual Mohican names associated with deed signings or witnessings in the Troy area and there appear to be at least 30 families or kinships involved in ownership. Between 1651 and 1708, most of the land that now comprises Troy and the surrounding areas was given up by the Mohicans in land deals with the Dutch. Land between the Poestenkill and Piscawenkill (present-day Middleburgh Street), which represents most of downtown and South Troy, was owned by the Mohican Annape.

The land that encompassed the Wyantskill and Poestenkill areas was owned by two Mohicans. The Wyantskill area was called Paanpack and was owned by Peyhaunet, while the area between the Wyantskill and Poestenkill, called Panhooseck, was owned by Aepjen (also known as Skiwias). From the Wyantskill south to North Greenbush (and an island obliquely eastward of present Menands), the land was owned by Pachquolapiet. Present-day Lansingburgh, known as Popgassik, was owned by Anaemhaenitt (Amenhamit).

Green Island, called Pachanhanit, or Nehanenesick, and a small island situated to the eastward was owned by Amanhanit, Aepjen, and Wanapet, and they sold it in 1665. Three islands in the Hudson River between the first and second forks of the Mohawk River, opposite "the Green Island," were owned by Ansinaneth and Squischecan. These are probably Starbuck's or Center Island (also known as Big Stoney and Fish Island), Hay Island, and Pompey or Adams Island. A small island known as Round Island, of 5 or 6 acres, near Green Island, with a freshwater brook on each side, was deeded in 1665, but the owner is not known. Today's Van Schaick Island, called Quahemesicos by the Mohicans and commonly known by name Long Island by the Dutch, was deeded over by Hamenet (Itamenet), Anemhameth (Amenhamit), and Knaep, also in 1665. The land around Cohoes including the falls was called Turkeyan by the Dutch and Nachawinasick by the Mohicans; it was owned by Apananos and his wife, Sowasqua. An island "situated between Cahoos and the plowed land of Turkeyan" was owned by Amenhamit and Aioot. This may have been Peebles Island. Before the construction of the Federal Dam and the filling in of the west branch of the Mohawk, which ran through Green Island and Watervliet and discharged opposite Broadway in Troy, there were several other islands in the river, but they are now filled in or submerged.

All of this land was eventually sold to the Dutch. What did the Mohicans get in return? According to the deeds, land was sold for rugs, muskets, kettles, gunpowder, bars of lead, fur caps, shirts, strings of wampum, strings of tobacco, a child's coat and shirt, knives, hatchet, adze, pouches, socks, duffel coat, beaver, bread, beer, a piece of cloth, a cutlass, axes, jugs of rum, blankets, duffel coats, guns, Madeira wine, pipes, and five shillings. Some would say today that it wasn't a very good trade.

A group of Mohicans, then "christianized," left the area and founded Stockbridge, Massachusetts, but even there, their days were numbered. After the loss of nearly half of the male Mohican population during the American Revolution (they sided with the colonists), the Oneida Indians, who had also fought for the colonists, offered the "Stockbridge" people a portion of their land on which to live; they settled it in the 1780s.

Again, this rich fertile land was taken by the white settlers, and the Mohicans migrated to the White River area in Indiana to live with their relatives, the Miami and Delaware. By the time they arrived, the Delaware had already been cheated out of their land.

Negotiations for a large tract of land in Wisconsin was initiated by the federal government, New York officials, and others, with the Menominee and Winnebago tribes, and the Mohicans began building a new village at Grand Cackalin called Statesburg. The treaty in 1822 allowed the Stockbridge and another group called the Munsee of the Delaware Confederacy in New Jersey to move, but the Menominee did not like the agreement and renegotiated. Finally, the Mohicans and Munsee moved to two townships on the east shore of Lake Winnebago by 1834. Another treaty in 1856 saw the Stockbridge and Munsee move to the townships of Bartelme and Red Springs in

The "Muh-he-kun-ne-tuk" (where the waters were never still) is now called the Hudson River. Troy has grown and prospered on the floodplain of the Mohican's river for more than 200 years.

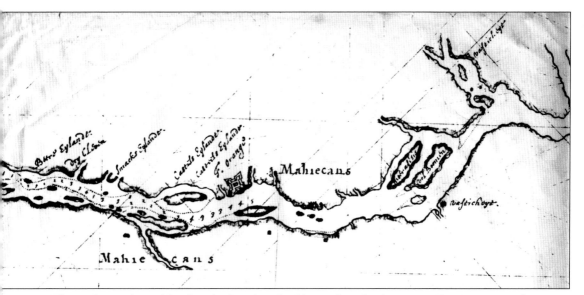

The Mohicans loaned land to the Dutch to build a trading fort known as Fort Nassau and later Fort Orange, now the present-day Albany. This was the first Dutch settlement in the region, which then spread to Schenectady to the west and to the Troy area to the north.

Shawano County. The official name of the groups became the Stockbridge-Munsee Band of Mohican Indians.

The 1934 Indian Reorganization Act made it possible for the Stockbridge Munsee people to reorganize their tribal government and get back some of the land that had been lost to unscrupulous lumber dealers. About 15,000 acres of land in the township of Bartelme were purchased for the tribe.

Contrary to James Fenimore Cooper's *The Last of the Mohicans*, which with one stroke of the pen exterminated these people from the minds of the public, the Mohican Nation, Stockbridge-Munsee Band, are doing just fine today.

3. LAND DEALS

In 1629, Kiliaen Van Rensselaer, a jewelry designer from Holland and a director of the Dutch West India Company, began the process of obtaining a land grant for the lands surrounding Fort Orange (Albany). The Dutch West India Company had devised a plan to encourage settlement of the area by promising anyone that would pay for the transporting of at least 50 adults that they could have land with government control similar to the old feudal system. These land barons would become "patroons," and their land tracts were called "colonies."

Land grants to the patroons were in the form of a tract 16 miles from the river on one side, or half of that on both sides. In Van Rensselaer's case, it extended on both sides of the river, covering an area that now encompasses Albany, Rensselaer, and part of Columbia Counties, and north and south of Fort Orange. By controlling the land around Fort Orange, Van Rensselaer gained control over Albany's future growth and trade.

Van Rensselaer's first purchase from the Mohicans took place on August 13, 1630, and included the land where Albany now sits. A few weeks later, he stretched the purchase to lands that went as far north as Monemius Indian Castle on Peebles Island (Waterford area), encompassing the west side of the river. The east side tract was later purchased by Van Rensselaer's agents on August 8 and 13, 1630, and included the land from Poetanock, near Castle Island, north to Negagonse, 12 miles up the river. Van Rensselaer went into partnership with John de Laet (a historian), Samuel Godyn, and Samuel Bloommaert.

Van Rensselaer's manor system was designed so that anyone could rent parcels but not own them. Renters were required to make an annual payment that could be in the form of beaver or wampum, or one-tenth the amount of grain raised, or one-half of the increase in animals or products cultivated, or wood, or even a number of days of labor. Furthermore, all surplus grain and cattle had to be offered to the patroon's agents first, and all grain grown had to be ground at the patroon's own mill. Van Rensselaer did give the tenant livestock, a house, and a barn to get started.

The area of Troy was depicted on a map drawn by Gillis Van Schendel in 1630, and he labeled the area Pafraets Dael (Part), which some historians interpreted as "the paradise of a lazy man," or "a lazy man's paradise," or "a lazy man's inheritance," or, finally, "a lazy crew's land." It may have simply been named in honor of Van Rensselaer's mother, Maria, whose maiden name was Pafraets.

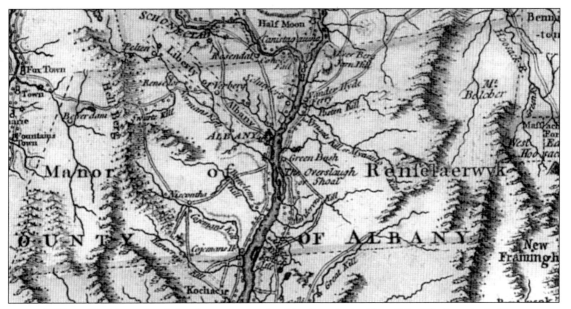

Kiliaen Van Rensselaer's land patent contained land on both sides of the Hudson, including the Troy area. Claims against the patent shown in this c. 1776 map were not settled until the late nineteenth century.

It appears that the first tenant (and non-native) to settle on what is now Troy territory was Thomas Chambers, a carpenter. On September 7, 1646, he signed a five-year contract with the officers of Rensselaerwyck.

The land had been purchased by Van Rensselaer's agents on March 13, 1652, from the Mohican owners. It lay between the Wyantskill and the Poestenkill and was divided between two Mohican owners. The land stretching from the Wyantskill north belonged to a Mohican named Peyhaunet and was called Paanpack (the "Great Meadow"), while the land that stretched from the land of Peyhaunet north to the Poestenkill and between the two creeks "as far land inwards as the Wappennakvias or else to the Sweet River" was the property of Skiwias. It was called Panhooseck. Peyhaunet and Skiwias (also called Aepjen), chief of the Mohicans, both signed the deed.

The previous year, on January 27, 1651, the patroon's agents purchased from the Mohican Pachquolapiet, in the presence of Aepjen, much of South Troy and North Greenbush from the Wyantskill, "south of the farm of Thomas Chambers, with the surrounding woods, and the adjoining land extending south to an Indian castle," and an island obliquely eastward of present Menands.

Thomas Chambers had rented this land between the Wyantskill and Poestenkill. In his lease, he was responsible for building his own house and barn, but he received two mares, two stallions, and four cows as part of the arrangement. Chambers also had first rights to erect a sawmill on one of the mills. He occupied the land from 1647 to July 14, 1654, when he surrendered the property and moved to Esopus. Chambers is credited with introducing into the colonies the use of clapboards on homes, a practice not known in Holland at the time, and his nickname became "Clabbordt," a corruption of the English clapboard.

The land was then leased to Jan Barentsz Wemp, also known as Poest (the Poestenkill is named for him), in 1654 for a period of three years. His rent was in the form of money (guilders), wheat, and oat. In 1659, he purchased from the Mohicans the land on the north side of the Poestenkill "beginning from the mill on the creek and to goe over the sd: Creek unto the great meadow ground whereabout sixty six paces the trees are markt." This covered most of Troy (excluding Lansingburgh) today. Wemp lived there with his wife, Maritie Mynderse. He died in 1663, and the following year, his wife married Sweer Theunisz Van Velsen, who was a former farmhand of Jan Barentson.

The land was subdivided and sold by Van Velsen. Peter Adriaens, who purchased a piece of the land, conveyed it on February 11, 1669, to his son Pieter van Woggelum. Owing a debt to Geertruyt Barents, wife of Jacob Heven, he gave up two lots. He left for Schenectady in 1669 and left the property, including the mill on the Poestenskill, to Jacob Heven. On October 18, 1674, Geertruay Piertese van Woggelum sold her interest in another sawmill on the second hill southward to Wyant Gerritse van der Poel (the Wyantskill is named for him).

Situated between the Wyantskill and Poestenkill was a farm owned by Jeronimus Ebbink, husband of Madam Johanna de Laet, heiress of John de Laet, a historian and one of Van Rensselaer's original partners. Madam de Laet also owned a brickworks in Albany that was recently uncovered by archaeologists and then destroyed for a parking garage. This farm was sold to Jurien Teunisse Tappen on July 7, 1667; he sold it on November 6, 1677, to Captain Philip Pieterse Schuyler and his wife, Margaret Van Slichtenhorst, who were early bearers of the Schuyler family name that would more than once be written in history. More land was sold to Peter Van Woggelum by Van Velsen on May 6, 1679.

Farther north, Lansingburgh was known as Tascamcatick by the Mohicans but known as Stone Arabia by the Dutch, perhaps due to the abundance of gravel and stones in the soil. In May 1668, Robert Sanders and Harmen Vedder obtained a farm at present-day Lansingburgh with the use of the woodland Popgassik, as named by the Mohicans, south of the farm, as free range for their cattle. Sanders received a patent for this land by Governor Francis Lovelace on September 1, 1670. The Dutch relinquished control of New Netherland to the English in 1664. Several years later, on December 30, 1678, Sanders purchased outright the woodland south of his farm extending down to the line of Peter van Woggelum, and also Whale Island, in the Hudson River, with a patent from Sir Edmund Andros.

Sanders, in turn, sold the land to Johannes Wendell, a farmer from Albany County on May 26, 1683. Wendell picked up additional land that went as far north as the present Troy-Waterford Bridge. Wendell and his son Robert held the property for some 80 years; however, they sold a northern portion on June 21, 1763, to Abraham Jacob Lansing. The lands purchased, which comprise most of present-day Lansingburgh, ran from the Piscawenkill to the Paensickill near the Waterford Bridge. Exceptions to this deal were the south portion of Stone Arabia, which was sold to Peter Van Woggelum, mentioned already in 1681, and a tract already sold to Simon Van Antwerp (though in the possession of William Rogers).

Abraham Jacob Lansing's property was a 5,000-acre farm. In 1771, only eight years after obtaining it, Lansing laid out his land into a square of 2 by 1.5 miles with 288 building lots, streets, alleys, and an oblong village green in the center. He named his new proposed city Lansingburgh. Instead, it became known as "Niew Stadt," or New City, as opposed to Albany, or "Old City," south of it. Lansingburgh quickly grew into a thriving village thanks to an influx of New England entrepreneurs.

By the end of the seventeenth century, several families were living along the Hudson River flood plain from the Wyantskill to Lansingburgh. By the end of the Revolutionary War, Troy was still an area of only a few farms, but that would soon change.

TALES OF THE POESTENKILL

Just west of Pawling Avenue, Mount Ida Falls, a remnant of the last glacial episode that covered the valley some 15,000 years ago, smashes its water among the ancient rocks. The falls is part of the mighty Poestenkill, which flows west from the hills and tumbles some 220 feet above the city, carving its way through bedrock as it discharges its water into the Hudson below. This beautiful stream and valley played an important part in the industrial development of Troy during the nineteenth century. It also has been a source of scientific study, legend, and lore, and a favorite recreational site for Trojans for hundreds of years.

This nineteenth-century view of Mount Ida Falls shows the bridge that once spanned the gorge.

Not far from the stream was the Dutch homestead of Richard Vaughn, who had a beautiful daughter named Elsie. It was quite common in the early settlement years for Mohawk Indians to visit the Dutch settlers in the area, for it was a time of mutual respect and cooperation.

One young Mohawk warrior named Dekanisora fell in love with Elsie, but the love was not returned. One night, as the story goes, when Richard Vaughn was away on

Ten-year-old Christopher stands at the mouth of the 600-foot Marshall Power Tunnel in the Poestenkill, which is used to supply power to several mills.

business, the young Mohawk broke into the home to carry Elsie away as a bride. His better judgement prevailed, but a few days later, he followed Elsie as she wandered along the stream and climbed on top of a ledge next to the falls.

Elsie fell asleep on the ledge, no doubt from the hypnotic effect of the falls, but was awakened suddenly and just in time to see the young Dekanisora save her life by killing a snake that had coiled and was poised to strike. Dekanisora then fell to his knees and professed his love for Elsie.

Elsie made it clear to the lovestruck warrior that she did not love him, but he was determined to take her. Not wanting to live a life in captivity, Elsie jumped from the ledge to her death. Dekanisora carried her lifeless body to "Robbers' Cave" for burial.

Shortly after returning from New York, Richard Vaughn died of a broken heart, never having recovered from the loss of his only daughter. Years later, when constructing improvements on the stream, young men found the cave and a few bones inside it. On one of the bones was the inscription, "Elsie."

The natural history of the gorge soon changed as early Trojans began to look for a source of waterpower. As early as 1667, a small sawmill was located on the west end of the gorge and was probably owned by Jan Barentsen Wemp. The power of the stream and its falls soon gave way to the building of several industries. By 1830, there were sawmills, gristmills, paper mills, and cotton mills all situated along the north bank of the stream. In 1840, Benjamin Marshall harnessed the power of the stream by drilling a 600-foot tunnel through the solid rock to provide power to his cotton factory and other mills along the stream.

Above the falls, a dam created the large Bleach Works (now Belden's) Pond to furnish waterpower for the Excelsior Knitting Mill on the north bank, just east of the dam. Under various names, the mill lasted until 1909.

It seems like poetic justice today that a hurricane—another part of Mother Nature— destroyed the dams and many of the mills in 1932, marking the end of the use of the valley as an industrial site. The harnessed power of the Poestenkill came to a final end when the last factory, Manning Paper Mill, burned in 1962.

The "gorge," as it is known, was a favorite place to picnic during the nineteenth century. A small, unobtrusive bridge crossed the gorge just below the falls so that people could explore both sides of the stream. Fishing, swimming, and picnicking were favorite pastimes and continue to be today.

To the nineteenth-century geologist, the gorge became the site of the discovery of the famous rock thrust, first known as the Logan Fault. This thrust slope begins in Canada and runs down to Alabama. Here in the gorge one can see older rock deposits of the Cambrian period (500 million years ago) resting on top of earlier ones of Ordovician age (350 million years ago). It is now called the Emmons Thrust after Ebenezer Emmons, graduate of RPI's first class and first junior professor.

4. Almost Troy

The mighty oak tree, which stands tall, provides shade for wildlife, and produces lumber sought after by woodworkers everywhere, gets its start from a simple, small acorn. Troy also had similar modest beginnings. On June 2, 1707, Derick (or Dirck) Vanderheyden, the son of Jacob Tysse Vanderheyden of New Amsterdam (New York City), purchased two tracts of land from Pieter Van Woggelum that encompassed land from the Poestenkill to the Meadow Creek (near Hoosick Street). During most of the eighteenth century, the area now called Troy was farmland under the control of the Vanderheyden family.

Derick Vanderheyden had three sons: Jacob, David, and Mattys. On November 1731, he deeded his farm to all his sons, giving each equal thirds. David sold his interest in the farm to brother Jacob in 1732, apparently having no interest in the land.

Founder Derick's son Jacob had two sons of his own, Dirck and Jacob. Dirck had a son named Jacob D. Vanderheyden, who had a son named Jacob I. Vanderheyden. Mattys Vanderheyden, the third son of the original owner, Derick, deeded his portion of the land to his sons Dirck and John and his grandson Matthias Vanderheyden, the son of Dirck. In essence, the three Vanderheydens who were to found Troy as we know it today were the great-grandsons of the original owner, Derick.

Jacob and Mattys created a partition deed on April 3, 1789, dividing the farm into three parts. Jacob retained title to the middle and northern sections, and Mattys received the southern part. When Jacob died on April 18, 1764, his son Dirck became owner of the middle and northern farms, but on July 2, he deeded over the northern portion to his brother Jacob.

Finally, Jacob I. received the northern portion by a deed from his father. Brother Jacob D. became owner of the middle farm when Dirck died on May 11, 1774. Matthias became sole owner of the southern farm when his father, Dirck, died on March 1, 1770, or he may have already had ownership deeded from his grandfather Mattys.

Confused yet? The final ownership of the land shortly before it became Troy was three farms owned by Jacob D. (1758–1809), Jacob I. (1750–1801), and Matthias Vanderheyden (1760–1825). The northern farm was bounded on the north by Piscawenkill (now buried near Ingalls and Middleburgh Streets) and on the south by Grand Division Street (now called simply Grand). It was surveyed and mapped by John E. Van Alen on February 8, 1793. The middle farm was bounded on the north by Grand Division Street and on the south by Division Street. It was surveyed and mapped by Flores Banker on May 1, 1787, and by John Van Alen on September 10, 1801. The southern farm was bounded on the north by Division Street and on the south by the Poestenkill. It was surveyed and mapped by John E. Van Alen on May 10, 1793.

Early records tell us that the northern and middle farms were more productive than the southern farm. Land between Ferry and Division Streets was fenced and tilled. Orchards were on the bank of the river near River Road (present River Street), and at the foot of the hills around Fifth and Sixth Avenues stood forests of pine and scrub oak, part of the extensive pine barrens region that covered most of Albany, Schenectady, and Rensselaer Counties (locally called the Pine Bush).

Jacob I. Vanderheyden lived in a small one-story brick house (later expanded) just past Hoosick Street on River Street. Floors planks were 10-inch yellow pine (pitch pine) fastened to 12- to 14-inch oak beams. Room height was not more than 8 feet. This building was later converted and connected to the Seton Day Home on nearby Fifth Avenue and was standing until the late 1970s, when it was demolished. The site is now paved, but part of the hand-wrought fencing is still visible on River Street.

Jacob D. Vanderheyden, called the patroon, lived in a framed building on the southeast corner of River and Ferry Streets, a site now occupied by a Russell Sage Dorm. He later

JACOB I. VAN DER HEYDEN'S HOUSE. 1756,
Location 548 River St. between Hoosick & Vanderheyden Sts.

Jacob I. Vanderheyden's home was standing until the 1970s. It is now a parking lot.

built a larger brick house on the southwest corner of Grand Division and Eighth Street. This building was also destroyed in recent times.

Matthias Vanderheyden lived in a two-story house on the southeast corner of Division and River Streets. It too is a parking lot today and is owned by Russell Sage College.

While the remains of Jacob D. Vanderheyden's homes are probably obliterated, the home sites of Jacob I. and Matthias could be excavated, artifacts recovered, and preserved as memorials to Troy's early founders.

Matthias Vanderheyden's house was standing until the late nineteenth century, when it was demolished for a steam engine company. The site is now a parking lot.

5. It Takes a Village

By the 1750s, there were about a dozen people living in the Troy area. Two roads originally led out from Derick Vanderheyden's house. One went north, following most of the course of present-day River Street and then split, with one end continuing north and the other spur heading east up to Schaghitcoke. North First Street from King Street to North Street follows this path today and may be the only original part of this historic road left. The second road from Vanderheyden's house went northeast to Hoosick.

By Revolutionary War times, several farms along the river were occupied by Abraham Lansing, William Rogers, the Vanderheydens (Jacob I., Jacob D., and Matthias), a "Widow Magin," Jan Van Beuren, Cornelius Van Beuren, Philip Wendell, and others. One of these settlers—Abraham Jacob Lansing—wasted no time subdividing his land into building lots.

Abraham Jacob Lansing originally established the area that encompasses Lansingburgh (present-day North Troy), originally called Tascamcatik by local Native Americans, in 1763 as a 5,000-acre farm. This was part of the original Stone Arabia Patent, owned by Robert Wendell Jr., and a portion was sold to Lansing for 300 pounds.

Only eight years later, in 1771, Lansing hired Albany surveyor Joseph Blanchard to lay out his land into a rectangle of about 1,300 by 2,000 feet with 288 building lots, streets, alleys, and an oblong village green in the center. However, there is evidence he laid out lots near the river earlier since he sold several lots to individuals as early as 1770.

Lansing may have been encouraged to divide his land for two reasons. The original name, Stone Arabia, is evidence to the geography of the location, for the area was covered with coarse stone and gravel, and perhaps Lansing thought it would never be cultivatable. The second was pure speculation that the tide of emigration from New England would prove profitable.

Surveyor Blanchard laid out the new city "in a regular square for the erecting a city by the name of Lansingburgh." He went on to note on the map that "the Oblong Square in the Center is reserved for Public uses." Since the area was already known as Stone Arabia, it was wise to change the name of the new city since there already existed a Stone Arabia farther west. This could have confused early immigrants into moving to the wrong area. Regardless, Lansingburgh was now located in the town and borough of this new Stone Arabia.

What is most interesting about the layout of Lansing's new city is that it closely matches the layout of 1733 Savannah, Georgia. Savannah is perhaps the first city in colonial America to be laid out using alternating service alleys through every single block, as

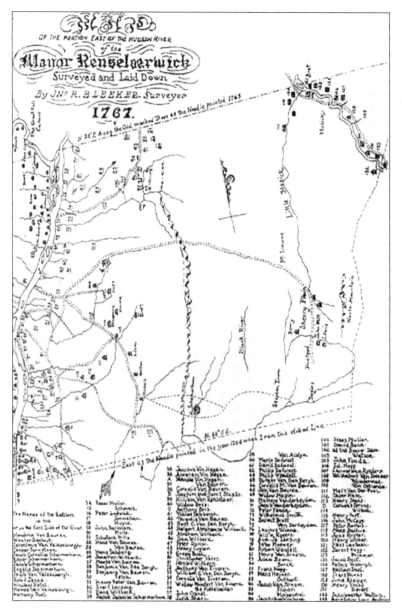

This map of the eastern part of the Manor shows several farms along the Hudson River in the Troy area by 1767.

pointed out by Albany historian John Wolcott. Lansingburgh's design closely mimics one of Savannah's blocks with a center public square, surrounded by evenly spaced blocks of streets and alleys, with a major street entering the center of the public square. This general design, with oblong blocks laid out in a uniform grid pattern, may have originated with the Greeks in the eighth century B.C. The grid system was often used when Greeks created colonies in other parts of the world. According to Wolcott, the street plans, especially the alleys, are the most significant colonial period relic that Lansingburgh has to show today.

While Lansing named his new proposed city Lansingburgh, it became known as "Niew Stadt," or New City, as opposed to Albany, which was "de Oude Stadt," or the old city, south of it. Lansingburgh quickly grew into a thriving village thanks to an influx of New England entrepreneurs, but the Dutch were still very much a factor.

Many New Englanders flocked to the newly created city and purchased lots from Lansing. Several lots were sold in 1770 before the official map was drawn up, indicating that there may have been an earlier unofficial map created. These early lots were sold to Robert Yates (lot 6), John Dunbar (81, 82, 152), Benjamin French (17, 18), Elinor Taylor (1, 2), Jacob A. Lansing (13, 216), Abraham Blaau (5, 21), Issac Lansing (65), Jonathan Wickwire (81), and Samuel Halstead (102).

In 1771, the year the official Lansingburgh map was drawn by Blanchard, the following people purchased lots: John Barber (240), Anne Hamersley (225, 233), Flores Bancker (169–183, 185, 186, 187–192, and water lot 25), Charles Meal (11), Anthony Rutgers

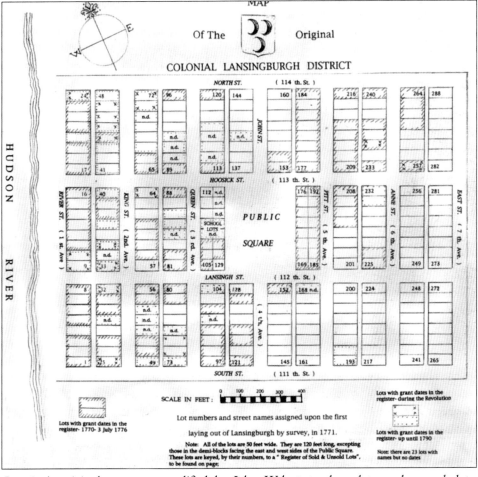

Lansing's original map was modified by John Wolcott to show lot numbers and dates before 1790.

(105, 129), Evert Banker (113), Peter Curtinus (8), Alex McClean (7, 257), Waldron Blaau (5, 184), Jonathan Brewer (66, 212), Eldart Funda (5), John D. Funda (97–99), Mayekie McCoy (213), and Issac I. Lansing (27, 51). Seventy-one other individuals purchased lots from Lansing by 1790, when records cease to exist.

Four lots were created for the establishment of public schools (108, 109, 182, 183). As early as 1774, a school was erected by Maus R. Van Vranka, who also agreed to read a sermon in English and Dutch every Sunday but four.

The local government of Stone Arabia, or Lansingburgh, was a curious mixture of democracy and oligarchy. A committee of five people was elected each year along with the offices of moderator, town clerk, path master, and three fence viewers. The arrangement agreed upon was that there always would be a member of the Lansing family (Abraham Jacob or one of his heirs) as one of the five committee members.

The first officers of the town in 1771 were Ebenezer Marvin as moderator, Thomas S. Diamond as clerk, and committee members Jacob A. Lansing, Isaac Bogart, John Barber, Ebenezer Marvin, and Benjamin French. Abraham Wendell was the path master. Robert Wendell, Levinus Lansing, and Isaac Van Arnum were fence viewers.

Almost a decade after the layout of the city, Elkanah Watson, while surveying for the location of a western canal, visited Lansingburgh and wrote the following:

The Burgh's public square was used by residents for a variety of events, including as a parade ground for Revolutionary War troops.

Northwestern view of Lansingburg.

This engraving shows Lansingburgh as a thriving riverfront business community in 1841.

I spent a day in examining this locality [speaking of the Troy area] and then walked on the banks of the Hudson, a distance of three miles to New City, where I continued several days. This place is thronged by mercantile emigrants, principally from New England, who have enjoyed a very extensive and lucrative trade, supplying Vermont and the region of both banks of the Hudson, as far as Lake George, with merchandise; and receiving in payment wheat, pot and pearl ashes and lumber.

The "Burgh," as its called today, was annexed to the City of Troy in 1900, but present-day residents of Lansingburgh still have a deep sense of a separate identity and their own claim to fame. Lansingburgh has contributed to national politics, literature, and sports while a separate village. For purposes of this book, the Burgh will be included as the city of Troy, except where otherwise noted.

The products of early Lansingburgh industries in oilcloth, brush making, valves, knit goods, beer, crackers and biscuits, scales, carriages, and shirts and collars were world famous during the nineteenth century and continued to be so even after the village became part of the City of Troy.

On April 17, 1775, 46 of Lansingburgh's leading inhabitants signed a proclamation opposing England's rule, possibly the first declaration of independence signed in the country, a year before the colonies' historic July 4, 1776 proclamation.

Chester A. Arthur, 21st president of the United States, lived and was educated in Lansingburgh and taught locally at Schaghitcoke and Cohoes. His father was a well-

Diamond Rock afforded the general public a picturesque view of the Hudson Valley for hundreds of years before it was occupied by a residential development.

known local preacher. Famed novelist Herman Melville, best known for *Moby Dick*, also spent his youth here. Melville's boyhood home, now the Lansingburgh Historical Society, is the location in which he wrote his first two novels. George R. Poulton, also from Lansingburgh, composed the song "Aura Lee," which became the melody for Elvis Presley's "Love Me Tender." A colorful character, Poulton was tarred and feathered for having an affair with a young student.

A part of American baseball history also began in Lansingburgh. The Union Haymakers, an early Lansingburgh baseball team, later became the New York Giants, now located in San Francisco. Four of the Union ballplayers are in the Baseball Hall of Fame.

The Lansingburgh Academy was an important educational institution that lasted 150 years. To this day, Lansingburgh still maintains its own separate school district.

Even though Lansingburgh had become a thriving mercantile village on the river by the nineteenth century, the Vanderheydens to the south were in no hurry to divide up their farms just yet.

A VIEW FROM THE HILL

Just east of Lansingburgh and overlooking it is a rock outcrop rising more than 300 feet above sea level. Known as Diamond Rock, this stone outcrop is one of the Capital District's most famous natural landmarks. Various geological reports list quartzite, limestone, sandstone, and shale as the ingredients, but on a sunny day Diamond Rock sparkles like a diamond from the imbedded quartz crystals found in veins throughout the stone monument.

Standing on top of this summit, one can see the confluence of the Hudson and Mohawk Rivers and more than 100 miles up and down the Hudson Valley—a view that includes the Catskill Mountains on the south and the Adirondacks on the north. This is a view so beautiful that historian John Wolcott recalled that the well-to-do Albany trader John Sanders, who owned much of the land that is now Lansingburgh in the seventeenth century, made it a point to take missionary travelers Dankers and Sluyter to the top for a visit in 1679–1680.

For hundreds of years, local inhabitants and visitors from around the world enjoyed picnics and sightseeing on Diamond Rock. Even Gypsy families called it home once in a while. Fireworks were set off there during celebrations such as Troy Week in 1908.

But today, Diamond Rock is private property for the most part, with housing and commercial developments sprinkled on top, and no longer the haven for those who want to commune with nature. Sadly, it is one more example of the chipping away at the features that made Troy so different from the rest of the world—both in terms of natural and human history.

There is a great Indian legend about Diamond Rock and how those "diamonds" (Herkimer Diamonds, really double-faced quartz crystals) were formed. It is called the "Legend of Diamond Rock" or "The Old Indian's Story of Moneta." This legend was told to Nathanial Sylvester and published in 1877.

The story goes that a Mohican village covered the flood plain on the east side of the Hudson just opposite the mouth of the Mohawk (probably near Freihofer) and was led by a chief named Hohadora. The chief lived there with his wife, Moneta, and two sons, Onosqua and Taendara. Onosqua was captured in the north and saved from torture by being adopted by an Adirondack Indian woman who had lost her own son at battle. Hohadora made several attempts to recapture his son, all failing. On his deathbed, Hohadora instructed his other son, Taendara, to recover Onosqua, or his remains, and bury him next to his father and mother. The village members would take care of Moneta during his absence.

Each night Moneta started a fire on top of Diamond Rock so that Taendara would see the light and find his way home. Each night for the next 20 years she sat by the fire crying, her tears falling around her, waiting for her sons to return.

Finally, Taendara, carrying his brother's bones, climbed the summit to reunite with his now aged mother, and as they embraced, they were struck by lightning. The next morning when the Indian villagers visited the site, the bones of Onosqua lay on the ground, but Moneta and Taendara were gone. The bare ground sparkled with Moneta's tears—20 years' worth—all of which were turned into diamonds by the force of the lightning.

Diamond Rock, like Moneta and Taendara, is gone now, at least in the public sense. On top of Diamond Rock are developments like "Terrace at High Pointe," complete with roadways like Ridge Circle, Outlook Court, Woods Path, and Diamond Rock Circle.

6. VANDERHEYDEN'S VILLAGE

The Vanderheydens were not blind to the amassing fortunes of nearby Abraham Lansing and his "new city." Jacob I. Vanderheyden was the first to capitalize on the possibility of economic fortune. He sold a lot on the west side of River Street, 485 River, near Hoosick Street, to Benjamin Thurber, who was originally from Providence, Rhode Island. Thurber erected a frame building, filled it with merchandise, and hung a sign outside in the style of a bunch of grapes that advertised his wares.

Thurber was followed by Captain Stephen Ashley of Salisbury, Connecticut. Ashley took a two-year lease on the old Matthias Vanderheyden house at the corner of Division and River Streets and opened it as a tavern. He also had ferry rights and operated the only ferry, which soon became known as Ferry Hook or Ashley's Ferry, in the area.

In 1786, Benjamin Covell from Providence, Rhode Island rented a building from Ashley and opened a store. He made more money in one day ($20) than he did working a whole week in Providence.

Jacob D. Vanderheyden, apparently waking up to the fortunes his relatives Jacob I. and Matthias were enjoying, decided to get into the fray. He hired surveyor Flores Bancker to lay out his middle farm into building lots, and the survey was completed on May 1, 1787. Upon the advice of an acquaintance of Vanderheyden, the survey was laid out based on the model of Philadelphia, a plan set in regular squares and rectangular streets. He named his new village Vanderheyden.

In 1788 Elkanah Watson, an Albany entrepreneur, visited and made the following prophetic observations:

> From Schenectady, I passed the road to Ashley's Ferry, six miles above Albany. On the east side of the river, at this point, a new town has been recently laid out, named Vanderheyden. This place is situated precisely at the head of navigation on the Hudson. Several bold and enterprising adventurers have already settled here; a number of capacious warehouses and several dwellings are already erected. It is favorable situated in reference to the important and growing trade of Vermont and Massachusetts; and I believe not only bids fair to be a serious thorn in the side of New City, but in the issue a fatal rival. I think Vanderheyden must, from its more eligible position, attain ultimate ascendancy.

In the following year, on January 5, 1789, the small but enterprising population of Vanderheyden landowners decided to change their name to Troy. They published their event in local newspapers claiming that "From its present improved state, and the yet more pleasing prospect of its popularity arising from the natural advantages in the mercantile line, it may not be too sanguine to expect, at no very distant period, to see Troy as famous for her trade and navigation as many of our first towns." Jacob D. Vanderheyden, not impressed with the choice of name, continued writing in deeds and other legal transactions "Vanderheyden, alias Troy."

Both the northern farm of Jacob I. and the southern farm of Matthias were surveyed and mapped by John E. Van Alen. In 1793, Van Alen resurveyed Jacob D.'s land as well. Troy was now ready to grow and even surpass New City (Lansingburgh), even though the latter village had a 30-year headstart on Troy. Troy was now a village of some size, and an influx of New Englanders began. By 1791, there were about 50 inhabitants and businesses.

Ebenezer and Samuel Wilson from Mason, New Hampshire had come to Troy on foot and begun making bricks using clay from Mount Ida. Sam Wilson later proved that his meat-packing ability would result in his likeness becoming a national symbol.

There may be no Santa Claus or Easter Bunny, but there is at least one cultural icon that is real—Uncle Sam. Fortunately for Troy, it was a popular businessman who became the symbol of a new emerging nation. The alternative for the city could have been "Home of Brother Jonathan."

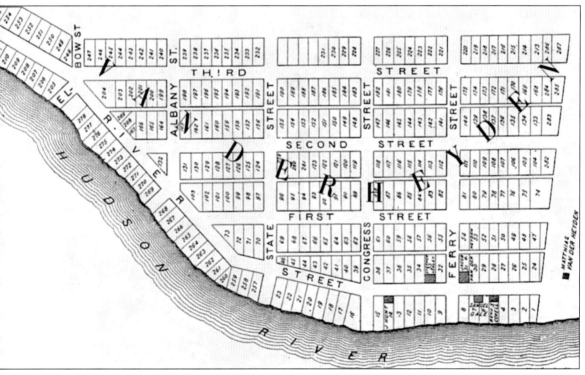

The new city of Vanderheyden was laid out in this way in 1787.

In the early part of the nineteenth century, America was known as "Brother Jonathan" to the inhabitants of the new country and to Europeans. Brother Jonathan appeared after the Revolution and seems to have been based on Jonathan Trumball, governor of Connecticut. George Washington relied on him for supplies and advice during the war, and would often mutter "We must consult Brother Jonathan on the subject" when contemplating action.

The English used the name as an insult (as they did Yankee Doodle), and it also came to symbolize the typical American to many overseas. Brother Jonathan became a sympathetic figure for early Americans after the war and even appeared in a Boston play in 1787, *The Contrast*. The character also appeared in music and cartoons of the period, which often showed him whittling, a favorite American pastime. However, it was the War of 1812 that changed the course of this American ethnoglyph.

In February 1789, Samuel and Ebenezer Wilson trudged on foot to the new village of Vanderheyden. Born in Massachusetts but raised in Mason, New Hampshire, the kids knew how to make bricks. The Wilson brothers started brickmaking at the west foot of Mount Ida at Sixth Avenue and Ferry. In 1793, they leased a lot from Jacob D. Vanderheyden on the northeast corner of Second and Ferry and built a small house. They also created a butcher business and built a large slaughter and packing house on the north bank of the Poestenkill. With more than 100 men working for them, they slaughtered more than 1,000 head of cattle a week.

Uncle Sam's house on Seventh Avenue and Ferry was torn down during the bicentennial.

About the same time, just south of Troy in Greenbush, the U.S. government purchased 300 acres and built barracks and a parade ground to house 6,000 troops, including Troy's own "Fusileers," "Trojan Greens," and "Troy Invincibles." It was not uncommon for these troops to pass through Troy on their way to the camp. Here, they would recuperate and eat. Large oak casks of salt beef and pork with the initials "U.S." were a common site.

Sam Wilson was known to his friends and family around Troy as "Uncle Sam," and he apparently had a very kind disposition. Sam and Ebenezer advertised as early as 1805 that they could butcher and pack 150 head of cattle a day. When the War of 1812 broke out, Sam secured a job as meat inspector for the Northern Army and also sought contracts to supply meat.

One of the accounts Sam inspected was Elbert Anderson's. Anderson had secured a one-year contract to supply all rations to troops in New York and New Jersey. In October 1812, he advertised for bids to supply 2,000 barrels of pork and 3,000 barrels of beef to be packed in barrels of white oak. The Wilsons got the job. The barrels were marked "E.A.-U.S.," referring to Anderson and the United States. But when asked what the initials meant, Wilson workmen said it referred to Elbert Anderson and Uncle Sam.

The name caught on since everyone in the area knew Uncle Sam Wilson and his wife "Aunt Betsey." In 1813, a broadside was printed with the first reference to Uncle Sam, and mention is made the same year in the *Troy Post*. Many periodicals carried the notion of Uncle Sam the following year, and it simply caught on. Today, the United States and Uncle Sam are one and the same.

Sam Wilson had a farm house at the junction of Cottage and Fifteenth Streets, and the area just north of Liberty and Division, at the end of Mount Ida, was called Wilson's Hollow. Later, Uncle Sam built a farmhouse at 177 Ferry, and he died there on July 31, 1854.

In early Troy, Mahlor Taylor from New Jersey had a saw and flour mill on the Poestenkill. Two former Revolutionary War soldiers, Colonels Albert Pawling and Abraham Ten Eyck, moved to Troy from Lansingburgh and set up a business. Pawling became Troy's first mayor a few years later. Jas Wardwell and George Young both had a blacksmith shop, Jacob Bishop operated a shoe store, and Adam Keeling had a leather store. A German cake and beer shop stood at the corner of Federal and King Streets. There were also two lawyers, John Woodworth and John Bird, ready to take care of legal work. Ananias Platt, an innkeeper, ran a stagecoach stop. Philip Heartt's saddlery and harness shop took care of the horses, and Captain Ashley and John Dickens both ran taverns. Ashley's famous sign above his establishment read, "This gate hangs high, it hinders none, refresh, then pay, and travel on." A school, shipyard, and church were built, and Jacob D. Vanderheyden even deeded a village green and burial place to the village.

On March 25, 1794, the legislature appointed Jacob D. Vanderheyden, Benjamin Covell, Anthony Goodspeed, John Pease, Ephraim Morgan, Christopher Hutton, and Samuel Gale as the first trustees of that part of Troy that was situated between the Poestenkill and Meadow Creek (near Hoosick), and a half mile eastward; basically, this was the original 1707 land grant to Derick (Dirck) Vanderheyden. Four years later, on February 6, 1798, the village of Troy was officially incorporated. Many Lansingburgh businessmen decided to move to Troy or at least set up a shop there as well.

Most of the earliest immigrants picked the middle farm of Jacob D. Vanderheyden on which to settle, although there were a few settlers on the northern farm lots of Jacob I. Vanderheyden and one or two on the south farm lots of Matthias. But it was clear that the land from Liberty to Grand Division was going to be home to the major hustle and bustle of the new village of Troy.

Part of this was due to the location of the middle farm at the head of navigation on the Hudson. All roads led westward to the ferry at the corner of River and Ferry Streets, and farmers from the Bought area (Cohoes), just west of there, found it easier to bring their produce there instead of to Albany or Lansingburgh. But there were other markets in Vermont, Massachusetts, and beyond that proved profitable to anyone who monopolized that trade with good roads.

Elkanah Watson helped stir up the issue of road improvements. Watson, an Albanian who believed in good infrastructure, was a supporter of the growing turnpike movement—toll roads owned by corporations. The turnpike idea was not new. Britain first authorized a toll-road in 1663, and "turnpike mania" swept England from about 1750 to 1772.

When a turnpike organizer in Albany could not arouse public interest, Watson wrote a series of articles in the Troy and Albany newspapers, baiting each town. In the Albany paper, he chastised readers for letting Lansingburgh and Troy attempt to monopolize the northern trade at their expense. In the Troy paper, he encouraged Trojans to build a turnpike connecting to Schenectady on the west. Additional articles finally produced the desired effect. Albanians were jealous and fearful that Troy would steal all the northern trade and the Schenectady Turnpike Company was created. But Lansingburgh wasn't sleeping either.

In 1799, Albany developed the Great Western Turnpike. Lansingburgh followed with the Northern Turnpike, and directly across from Albany, in Rensselaer, the Eastern Turnpike and the Rensselaer-Columbia (originally called the Albany-Columbia in 1798) Turnpike were created. By 1805, there were several turnpikes radiating out from the Albany and Troy area. Troy finally created the Troy-Schenectady Turnpike (1802), and Albany followed with the Albany and Schenectady Turnpike (1802) and the Albany-Delaware (1805). Whatever Albany did, Troy was to follow or vice versa.

Although New York was almost last among states promoting the turnpike (New York's full adoption of the turnpike plan came only with its General Law in 1807), the infrastructure for trade routes, along with river transportation, was now in place for the Capital District region. Turnpikes, however, were not the financial windfall that supporters thought they would be and most were unprofitable, not to mention unwelcome by local citizenry (who often used "shun-pikes"—free roads—to get around the toll gates).

From 1797 through 1846, 449 turnpike companies were incorporated in New York State, but the number of those that actually built roadways and collected tolls was only 165. Even the short-lived boom of plank roads between 1846 and 1853 did not help. Water routes (the Hudson River and the Erie Canal) and later steam (steam-powered boats and trains) killed the turnpikes eventually, but these two factors also helped Troy stand out from the rest.

The Troy-Albany Turnpike Toll House served for 50 years until December 11, 1913, when it burned. Owned by the Watervliet Turnpike and Railroad Company, the building was abandoned in 1905 when a movement to abolish tolls in the state began.

Another important factor that improved Troy's standing was its becoming the political seat for the newly created Rensselaer County on February 7, 1791. On March 18, the Town of Troy was carved out of Rensselaerwyck, and the village became part of the town. After much political posturing from both Lansingburgh and Troy to win the county seat, Troy won when their candidates for the state legislature were elected. Troy became the county seat in January 1794, when the first county courthouse and jail was built on the northeast corner of Second and Congress Streets. To this day, a county courthouse sits on that parcel.

On February 6, 1798, Troy incorporated as a village and boasted a population of about 1,500 people (now surpassing Lansingburgh in population). To say Troy grew quickly is an understatement. In 1800, only two years after incorporating, a local newspaper recorded the following:

> It will be sufficient for us to observe that fifteen years ago there were in this village (now comprising somewhat more than a mile square) but two dwelling houses, and probably not more than fifteen inhabitants, and that at the present time it contains about 300 dwelling houses (independent of stores, etc.) and 1,802 inhabitants. A population so rapid has, we believe, but seldom been witnessed in the United States.

In 1805, it was necessary to start placing wooden boards with hand-painted signs on the corners of buildings so that people could find their way. According to the 1806 *Troy Gazette*, most of the new construction was occurring along River, First, Second, and Third Streets in what is today downtown. There were several buildings on Fourth. Fifth Street (Avenue) had a few houses, and lots were also being purchased on Sixth Avenue.

When the English traveler John Lambert visited Troy in 1807, he made the following observation:

> Troy is a well built town, consisting chiefly of one street of handsome red brick houses, upwards of a mile and a half in length. There are two or three short streets which branch off from the main one; but it is in the latter [River Street] that all the principal stores, warehouses, and shops are situated. It also contains several excellent inns and taverns. The houses are all new and lofty and built with much taste and simplicity.
>
> The deep red brick, well pointed, gives the buildings an air of neatness and cleanliness seldom met with in old towns. The trade which Troy has opened with the new settlements to the northward through the states of New York and Vermont, as far as Canada, is very extensive, and in another twenty years it promises to rival the old established city of Albany. Its prosperity is indeed already looked upon with an eye of jealousy by the people of the latter place.

SOUNDS GREEK TO ME

It's all in the timing, as one philosopher said. Nothing could be more true when it comes to how Troy got its name. On January 5, 1789, the residents of Vanderheyden decided to change their community's name to Troy. Why? Some think it was because Troy was easier to write. Probably not!

To the Public.

THIS evening the Freeholders of the place lately known by VAN-DER HEYDEN's or ASHLEY's-FERRY, situate on the east bank of Hudson's-river, about seven miles above Albany, met for the purpose of establishing a name for the said place; when, by a majority of voices, IT WAS CONFIRMED, that in future, it should be called and known by the name of

TROY.

This advertisement that appeared in 1789 advised the public of their village's new name.

America had just won its freedom from England and there was a feeling of great democratic spirit throughout the country. Why not name their city after the country and cultural influence that created democracy—Greece? Moreover, a few years later, Greece herself was fighting for independence from the Turks (1821–1830), and the young America was sympathetic to her cause.

Troy was not alone in the adoption of the classics in name and style either. Many other cities in New York State followed suit: Athens, Attica, Ithaca, Ilion, Marathon, Syracuse, and Delphi, to name a few. Around 1818, this classical influence started showing up in architecture as well, and the Greek Revival Period (1818–1850) is considered the first truly national style in America. Even today, many of Troy's features and buildings remind us of our early classical beginnings.

One of the most famous Greek literary stories of the Trojan War is Homer's *The Iliad*. Part of *The Iliad* describes the wrath of Achilles at the action of Agamemnon,and tells the story of his withdrawal from the war. *The Iliad* was the inspiration for the archaeological work of Heinrich Schliemann in 1871, who discovered the site of Troy at Hissarlik, in modern Turkey. The New York city is named after that fabled city—a city that was rebuilt several times.

There are two geomorphic rises in Troy. Prospect Park, located between Congress and Hill Streets, rises 240 feet above sea level. It was named Mount Ida, which is also the name of the home of Zeus, the principal god of the Greeks. The other is Mount Olympus, which rises 100 feet above sea level and is located between Rensselaer, Vanderheyden, River, and Sixth. Actually, Fifth Avenue now runs through it. Mount Olympus is also the highest peak in Greece and the mythical home of all the Greek gods. In 1823, an octagonal building sat on top of Troy's Mount Olympus, serving cordials and beverages until it burned in 1830.

The well-known Cummings architectural firm of Troy designed the Ilium Building, located at the corner of Fulton and Fourth Streets. Ilium is another name for Troy.

The Lyceum was the name of the school outside Athens, Greece, where Aristotle taught between 335 and 323 B.C. A lyceum is a hall in which public lectures, concerts, and similar programs are presented. The Troy Lyceum of Natural History was organized in 1818 and was the first society of its kind. Many of the artifacts they collected were disbursed later to RPI and the Troy Library. St Peter's Lyceum was located on Hutton and Fifth Avenue. St. Peter's Church created it in 1885 as a social and athletic club.

Apollo Lodge, a Masonic lodge created in Troy on June 16, 1796, was named after the Greek god of music, medicine, and poetry. Apollo Hall was located in a building on the southeast corner of Congress and River Streets. This hall was used on Wednesday evenings by the Troy Turn Verein, a German fraternal society organized on August 8, 1852 (reorganized on September 30, 1885).

The Athenaeum building was located on First Street between River and State. It was built by the Troy Savings Bank in 1845 and torn down recently for a parking lot. It was named for The Athnaion, a Greek temple to Athena.

Greek influence did not end in the nineteenth century either. During the first quarter of the twentieth century, Greek immigrants found their way to Troy and opened restaurants throughout the city. Two such examples are the Famous Lunch on Congress Street and Hot Dog Charlie's in the Burgh; both are still serving customers.

49

The Approach was a grand entrance to the city from RPI when it was built, in Greek style, in 1908. The Ionic columns and lit staircase were built on the site of the former RPI main campus building, which burned.

Perhaps the most lasting examples of the city's fascination with the classics is in the architecture that bears the Greek name. Beginning in the 1820s, American architects were influenced by design books filled with buildings that were loosely based on ancient Greek temples. Probably the best examples of this Greek Revival architecture are found in local government buildings, but the style worked its way right down to single-family dwellings, and Troy has quite a few examples.

One of the more interesting examples of Greek Revival architecture is Cottage Row, a grouping of three small Greek temple–like homes that were built on the east side of Second Street between Liberty and Washington Streets around 1840. Designed with Ionic porticoes (a porch or walkway with a roof supported by columns) and built by carpenter Norton Sage, this Greek triplet was written up in *The Cultivator*, an Albany magazine, in 1843, and even included an engraving of the homes. The homes were separated from each other by a garden screen. Sage lived in the middle house and sold the other two. Aside from the removal of the garden screens, the replacement of the columns on one of the homes, and the erection of a three-story building between two of them, Cottage Row still exists as it did 159 years ago.

There are other examples of these little Greek temples scattered throughout the city. The address 274 Eighth Street was the 1840 home of Luther McCory, a merchant. Charles Lindley, a clerk at the *Troy Daily Whig*, lived at 163 Third Street in 1844. Joseph C. Taylor, a coppersmith, lived at 356 Third Street in 1838. John B. Lull lived at 549 Sixth Avenue (Lansingburgh) around 1840. John Moray lived at 819 Third Avenue (Lansingburgh) around 1845. Daniel Hudson, a tanner and furrier, lived at 358 Third Street around 1844. Many of these homes still exist and stand out from the surrounding homes.

Perhaps the most impressive example of Greek architecture now belongs to Russell Sage College. The First Presbyterian Church on the southwest corner of Sage Park was built in 1836. It is the oldest church building, of this denomination, in the city, although it no longer functions in that capacity. It is designed in Greek Doric Order similar to temples such as the temple of Poseidon at Paestum and the Parthenon in Athens.

TROY'S VILLAGE GREEN STILL GREEN

Troy still has its original Village Green. Seminary or Congress Park is a small parcel along Congress Street, bordered easterly by Second Street, westerly by First, and southerly by Russell Sage College. It has remained virtually the same for the past 200 years.

Troy received its first park even before incorporation. On May 10, 1796, two years before incorporation, Jacob D. Vanderheyden deeded over three lots, "bounded on the north by Congress Street, east by Second Street, south by Lot 115 and west by an alley," to be used as a public square. This original park was about half the size of the present one (extend the alley on Congress south through to Sage). Lot 115 was the site of Moulton's Coffee House, later used by Emma Willard for her Troy Female Seminary (Emma Willard School), and now Sage College. This deed also gave permission to construct "a public

The Athenaeum building, right, was the original home of the Troy Savings Bank. This building, including the YMCA, and the film shop on the left have been torn down for a parking lot.

schoolhouse or academy if judged proper by the inhabitants." They didn't build one. Vanderheyden received 5 shillings for the deal, roughly the weekly wage of a carpenter during Elizabeth I's reign, or the cost of about 15 pounds of candles. The other half of Seminary Park came from land owned by the First Presbyterian Church.

In 1792, a small wooden meeting house was built on the east side of First Street near Congress on land donated by Jacob D. Vanderheyden, a member of the church. The following June, the Reverend John McDonald delivered the first sermon at the new house of worship. A historic marker now rests on the site. A vault was built under the church, and the remains of Vanderheyden's mother and father were interred there. In 1795, Jacob D. deeded over three more lots to the church, lots 86, 87, and 88. In 1819, a small session-house was erected to the south of the meeting house.

On July 18, 1834, the church swapped land with the City. Lots 86, 87, and part of 86 were given to the City for lots 85 and 84, for the purpose of building a larger church. There was a small reservation placed on lot 86: "So that a small part of said meeting house so to be erected only shall stand upon said lots with a view that the residue of said lots may forever be kept open and kept unoccupied by any building and be enclosed as a public park and yard in front of the same meeting house."

It was also stipulated that the portico of the new church not extend into lot 86 by more than 15 feet. A right of way was also granted so that people could enter through Congress and First Streets: a gate to be placed on First, another on Congress, and another on either street west of the alley. Construction on the new church began in 1835. It stands today as a Greek Revival building that looks like the Parthenon, and is now owned by Russell Sage.

Over the years, the alley to the west was assimilated. Paths were created. Fences were erected and removed. Some landscaping occurred to prevent people from walking on the grass. Aside from the war memorial now there, and some benches, Seminary Park has remained one of Troy's emerald treasures for all citizens to use.

Seminary Park is pictured here in 1912. The First Presbyterian Church is to the right and behind it is Mouton's Coffee House, which later became Emma Willard's Female Seminary.

7. Troy Becomes a City

During the early years that Troy thrived as a village (1794–1815), the elected trustees spent much of their time developing the town's infrastructure. Trustee meetings often took place at the houses (inns) of Platt Titus, Howard Moulton, and Stephen Ashley. These village fathers raised taxes to build public markets, set the size of loaves of bread, purchased fire engines and houses, appointed a keeper of the public pound and a bell ringer, night watchman, and firemen. They instructed workers to drain ponds, build sewers, and improve and pitch streets. They even had time to license taverns (there were 10 in 1800) and set speed limits for horses and buggies. They also made it illegal for swine, horses, sheep, goats, geese, and dogs to run wild, or for kids to play ball in the village streets.

These improvements paid off in record time. In 1794, there were 450 people living in the village, and by 1815, there were 4,254 inhabitants.

On April 12, 1816, the New York legislature passed an act to incorporate Troy as a city. On May 14, the first charter election was held in the city's six wards and the first set of aldermen elected were George Allen (First Ward) and Amos Salisbury (assistant), Hugh Peebles (Second Ward) and John Loudon (assistant), Townsend McCoun (Third Ward) and Gurdon Corning (assistant), Stephen Ross (Fourth Ward) and Henry Mallory (assistant), Lemuel Hawley (Fifth Ward), and Philip Hart Jr. (Sixth Ward). The governor appointed Albert Pawling as mayor, and William L. Marcy as recorder.

The first quarter of the nineteenth century was a tremendous period of growth. P. Thomas Carroll, director of the Hudson Mohawk Industrial Gateway, commented that the rapid industrial rise of Troy and the inventiveness of its citizens made it the "Silicon Valley of the Nineteenth Century." Other historians call Troy the "Birthplace of the Industrial Revolution." These honors hold up, as Troy was an innovator in the production of iron and steel products and literally created the collar and cuff industry, all before 1850. If these two industries weren't important enough, Troy also became the center of American science during this period with the founding of the Rensselaer School (Rensselaer Polytechnic Institute), the first science college, led by the teachings of founder Amos Eaton, the school's first professor and the father of American geology. Education for women was not omitted either, as Emma Willard created the first female college, the Troy Female Seminary, in 1821.

All roads lead to Rome, as the old saying goes, but in the nineteenth century, many major events in American history were shaped by individuals from Troy, New York.

TROY'S HOLY CORNERS

You don't have to be religious to appreciate the architecture of Troy's churches and synagogues, particularly those built in the nineteenth century. As individual landmarks, they are works of art, often containing within their structures artifacts such as Tiffany windows or locally made Meneely bells. A church often stands out as the tallest structure in a neighborhood—letting everyone know that it is there if needed and reminding them that those tall spires or bell towers are just a bit closer to heaven.

At the turn of the century, Troy had over 70 churches, almost one church for every 1,000 people living in the city. There are about half of that today, and many are falling down from disrepair and lack of support. Troy still is a city of faith, but it is hard to maintain those buildings without a population to support them.

Troy received its first church when Jacob D. Vanderheyden gave the newly formed Presbyterian congregation three building lots on the south side of Congress Street fronting on First Street (now Seminary Park). In 1792, a plain wooden meeting house was built on the middle lot. Other denominations followed: Baptists, Methodists, Quakers, Protestants, Lutherans, Universalists, Catholics, and members of the Jewish faith, all built houses of worship throughout the city.

Most people think of religious institutions only as places of worship, but they served other important functions during Troy's industrial age. Most of Troy's population was working 12–15 hours a day, 6 days a week. Religious institutions offered a social safety net of support services to both the upper and working class, as well as the indigent.

Schools were an early benefit brought to Trojans. While many schools also ensured a good dose of religious training, the basic ABCs were taught, and in some, even degrees in higher learning were offered. St. Paul's Parish School was started in 1808 on the north side of the public market on the northwest corner of Third and State. In 1823, the Society of Friends (Quakers) built a schoolhouse on the corner of State and Fourth (State Street side) just down the street from St. Paul's. The School of Industry of St. Paul's was an outgrowth of the Mary Warren Free Institute, which started in 1815. This school taught poor girls how to sew and make their own clothes and later instructed vocals. In 1838, the Troy Episcopal Institute helped young men prepare for college. The short-lived Troy University organized by Methodists provided degrees in agriculture and civil engineering. La Salle Institute was organized in 1847 for Catholic boys. Many parochial schools were created in the nineteenth century and still exist today.

The Troy Hospital (St. Mary's) was founded by Catholic priest Peter Havermans as a result of his dealings with destitute and sick Irish immigrants in 1848. Another hospital, St Joseph's Maternity, was located in the remodeled home of the Sisters of St. Joseph on Jackson and Fourth Streets as late as 1923. Havermans also founded, in 1848, St. Mary's Female Orphan Asylum (later St. Vincent's Female Orphan Asylum), run by the Sisters of Charity, and the Troy Catholic Male Orphan Asylum in 1850.

In 1854, the Church Home of the City of Troy was formed by the Brotherhood of St. Barnabus as a house of mercy in a home at 5 Harrison Place and later Federal Street. This Episcopal-run home charged $300 for elderly ladies who wanted to become residents. A Presbyterian home for the aged was formed in 1871 on Fourth Street (where Proctors

St. Paul's Episcopal Church, on the corner of Third and State Streets, is pictured here c. 1900.

Theater is now). The Little Sisters of the Poor established a home for the indigent in 1875 on Hutton Street.

Mount Magdalen School of Industry and Reformatory of the Good Shepherd was founded in 1884 by the religious order of the Good Shepherd for wayward girls. The reformatory, part of which is now used as RPI's Incubator, was on Peoples Avenue. This same order ran the Guardian Angel Home and Industrial School next door.

Homeless infants were cared for by the St. Joseph's Infant Home, created in 1898 at Thompson and Mill Streets. Run by the Sisters of Charity, the Seton Home for Working Girls provided women with shelter in the old Jacob Vanderheyden home north of Hoosick Street. Even social clubs were created, such as St. Peter's Lyceum in 1885 and St. Joseph's Club in 1892.

In 1806, the Quakers of Troy rented and later bought a small house on the southwest corner of Fourth and State Streets for services. In 1874, the First Unitarian Church bought the property and built a large church. It was sold to St. Anthony's Roman Catholic Church in 1905, and they continue to own the site—that makes 193 years of religious ownership, more than 90 percent of the time that Troy has existed.

55

North First Street, part of the original River Road, is the only remaining native cobble stone street in the city.

TROY'S PUBLIC MARKET

At one time, there were three public market houses built by the city for its citizens. None exist today. According to historian Rutherford Haynor, those early markets were more than a place to get food, they were also part of a larger social event. Housewives met their friends or formed small groups and shared rumors and news. The buildings became a focal point for public forums by politicians and for religious meetings. Even concerts and plays were performed on the second floor above the fish, fruit, and veggies.

The first public market opened in Troy in March 1800 and was a wooden building 20 feet wide by 60 feet long. It sat in the middle of State Street between First and Second Streets. On the north and south sides of the building, underneath the overhanging roof, the Premier Engine Company, Troy's first fire department, hung their fire ladders and hooks, conveniently located in case of fire. This market served residents until 1806, when the village trustees sold it for $50.

That year, the city purchased land on the northwest corner of Third and State and built a new public market. It was known as Center Market, often referred to as "Cow Place," and another building was added to it in 1828. The solid building facing Third Street was used as a meat market while the open-air building on the north side of State Street was used for selling fish, vegetables, butter, and eggs. In 1860, the Arba Read firehouse was built on the site; a Fleet bank building is there now.

In 1812, the village trustees established two more markets. North Market was built on the south side of Federal Street in 1828. The next year the second floor was dubbed the Troy Theatre and opened on July 4 with a play called *Pizarro, or the Death of Rollo*. It was replaced by the Eagle Engine Company No. 10 firehouse, built on the site in the 1840s.

A house was built for the South Market in 1828 on the northeast corner of Division and Second Streets, but in August 1839, the City purchased two lots on the southwest corner, opposite the existing one. They erected a brick building, named it Washington Market, and opened it in May 1841. The second floor of this market was also converted into a theater.

In 1840, the City took the Troy Shipyard at the junction of River and Fulton Streets, earlier donated by Jacob Vanderheyden, and erected a brick building in Greek Revival style at a cost of $30,000. The first floor was rented to butchers and market men, and the large area on the second floor was used as a concert and lecture hall. Fulton Market opened in May 1841 at the same time as Washington Market. In February 1847, the hall on the second floor was turned into a theater and opened with the play *The Lady of Lyons* on Washington's Birthday. It burned in February 1903.

Even as public markets fell out of use, Trojans (the Women's Civic League, in particular) tried to revive them during the first quarter of this century. In 1910, the City developed a market place around Washington and Hill Streets and leased it to the Market Grower's Association, which lasted into the 1950s.

A MEMORIAL TO NORTH FIRST STREET

It's a fact that natural landscapes change over periods of time. The Troy of 10,000 years ago, for instance, was covered by glacial Lake Albany. But this is also true for human-created landscapes. Just north of the Green Island Bridge begins North First Street. No wider than an alley, this half-mile route runs parallel to and is slightly east of River Street, crossing Hutton, Hoosick, Vanderheyden, Jay, and Rensselaer, and ending at North Street. North First represents a classic piece of Troy's urban history. This cobblestone street was lined with the homes of working-class Trojans for more than 150 years.

North First is the last true cobblestone street in Troy. These are native cobblestones, not the granite or Belgium blocks commonly referred to as cobblestone. Native cobblestones are smooth, rounded stones produced by glacial activity and found at the bottom of ancient river or stream beds. Cobblestones were laid down on dirt streets and pounded together tightly to form a hard surface. The curbs were blocks of sandstone or shale.

Troy boasted in 1925 that 73 of 103 miles of streets in the city were paved: 22 miles of granite block, 20 miles of brick, 4 miles of wood block, and the rest of various products. Belgian block was introduced in 1854 (on First Street). Before this, streets were either dirt (with stone chips mixed in) or native cobblestone like North First.

North First is one of the "new" streets laid in Troy as it began its rise as an industrial center. Troy had just become a city only 20 years prior to it being "laid and pitched," probably around the same time as North Second and North Third Streets (Fifth and Sixth Avenues) in 1836. This began the development of the area called Middleburgh, which ran from Grand Division Street to the now buried Piscawenkill (Middleburgh Street). Basically, it was all the farm of Jacob I. Vanderheyden. Part of North First Street appears to be the original River Road, which ran from Dirck Vanderheyden's house on Ferry Street north past Jacob I. Vanderheyden's house, continuing north to Schaghitcoke.

In 1871, 121 Trojans lived at more than 40 addresses along North First. Add a good dose of children and you have a sizable population. These adults represented a range of working-class professions: bakers, boilermakers, brass and brush makers, carpenters, clerks, coach painters, drivers, an engineer, file cutters, furnace men, harness makers, masons, millers, molders, painters, porters, sash and shoemakers, stone cutters, teamsters, wagon makers, watchmen, general laborers, and 16 widows.

Forty were laborers, followed by carpenters (7), shoemakers (5), and teamsters (5) as the most common. With names like Kelly, Donohue, and Sullivan, it is clear that a large Irish population called North First Street their home. While walking this route, anyone with a good imagination can appreciate the hustle and bustle of neighborhood activity that occurred there.

In this c. 1880 view up Congress Street are many houses on Eighth Street, at top, that still exist. Most of the other buildings are gone. Fifth Avenue crosses Congress in the center.

The entire length of North First still survives, although much of it suffers from neglect. One can see evidence of cobblestones and stone curbs along the entire route, but except for one location, there is no evidence that a neighborhood ever existed. The small section south of Hutton where the street begins was called Rock Alley.

Only a few people lived there. Between Hutton and Hoosick, North First was later paved with yellow brick. The backs of two churches, a warehouse, and carriage house, are all one can see, with no evidence of homes. In 1871, 28 families were there.

Hoosick to Vanderheyden is altered. The back of a 1920s boarding house for working women can be seen. North First is paved up to Jacob Vanderheyden's lot, which is also paved and now a parking lot for the newly opened Standard building. Granite block pavement extends to Vanderheyden Street, mixed with natural cobblestone at the end. Apparently only five or so people lived on this stretch in 1871.

Vanderheyden to Jay is the most neglected. The Hoosick side is a parking lot, but cobblestones are evident on the south end and throughout. The street is filled with garbage and brush, making it almost impassable. There is no evidence of homes, but around 17 families did live there.

From Jay to Rensselaer is the best example of this historic cobblestone street. The northern portion (lots) up to Rensselaer is vacant, but it may become a parking lot soon. Around 17 families lived there.

Rensselaer to North Street is interesting. Remarkably, 170 North First still exists and is occupied by a retired worker—the last resident of North First Street. Jeremiah Hall, a shoemaker on River Street, owned and lived in this house in 1871 with a boarder Patrick Hall, a boilermaker.

Farther down, among the rubbish and an abandoned car, is some evidence of cobblestones. The westernmost part of Troy's famous Mount Olympus ends here and one can see the old Wheeler Brothers iron and brass foundry on top of it. Two frame buildings are near the end and may have been the northernmost homes on the street. North First ends at the Ale House on North Street.

Most of the history books that deal with Troy talk about the early layout of the three Vanderheyden farms being drawn in the "Philadelphia" style. Upon closer examination, this is not exactly true. Historian Arthur Weise stated that a friend of Jacob D. Vanderheyden suggested the Philadelphia style, which is nothing more than a grid of squares and rectangles with a center green.

In this sense, Troy is indeed laid out in the Philadelphia style, although there was no village green originally included, as there was in Philadelphia or Lansingburgh. Jacob Vanderheyden didn't get around to donating a village green until 1796. However, there definitely is a bit of Lansingburgh in Troy's design as well.

Considering that Troy and Lansingburgh were chief rivals, it is no wonder that in written histories of Troy very little reference is made to the northern neighbor. Yet, the layout of Troy with its service alleys had to be copied from Lansingburgh since the only other city with alleys was Savannah, Georgia, and it appears that this is the city plan Lansingburgh was based on.

8. SCIENCE AND EDUCATION

Before 1830, there were two important centers for the study of the science of geology: London, the largest city in the world at that time with 1,500,000 inhabitants; and Troy, New York, with a population of a little more than 10,000. In fact, before 1818, there was little published at all about American geology.

Several people are given credit for making Troy the birthplace of the study of geological science in America: Stephen Van Rensselaer (1764–1839), Amos Eaton (1776–1842), Silas Watson Ford (1848–1895), and Sidney Powers (1890–1932).

Stephen Van Rensselaer, a descendant of the original Dutch patroon Kiliaen, graduated from Harvard in 1782. In 1819, the New York legislature hired him to serve as president of the Central Board of Agriculture. Under the auspices of the board, two volumes were published (at Van Rensselaer's own expense) on the geology of Albany and Rensselaer Counties and were authored by Amos Eaton, a Columbia County native who originally trained as a lawyer. According to historians of geology, this was the first attempt in America to collect and arrange geological facts for the betterment of agriculture.

Amos Eaton had earlier conducted a geological survey in Massachusetts, and this survey is the first recorded instance of the American use of a field trip as a tool of study, a method that would later become the accepted way to train in public schools and colleges and remains a standard practice up to the present day. Also, in 1818, Eaton published a textbook with a time and rock classification and a local field guide that may be one of the first in the country.

Eaton's love of natural history was instrumental in helping to found the Troy Lyceum of Natural History in 1818, one of the first such natural history societies in the country. The Lyceum provided exhibits on natural history and published scientific papers until 1820, when Troy's first major fire destroyed most of its collections. It continued publishing in a scientific paper called *The Plough Boy* in Albany. In 1833, the Lyceum was provided with new space in the courthouse for its collections. But Eaton's glory really began when he teamed up with Van Rensselaer.

Van Rensselaer supported Eaton's geological study of the land adjoining the newly formed Erie Canal during the period 1823–1824. This survey revolutionized geology and other sciences through its introduction of new and precise nomenclature for the rocks of the state, according to the City University of New York's Dr. Gerald M. Friedman, the author of several papers on the history of American geology.

In 1824, Eaton asked Van Rensselaer for $300 to start the Rensselaer School (now Rensselaer Polytechnic Institute, or RPI), the first in America dedicated to the study of science. Van Rensselaer eagerly donated the money and financially supported the school until 1829. By 1830, Eaton, the founder and first professor of the school, had published a textbook and geologic map of the entire state, but was also making an enormous impact by becoming the mentor of several students who would later contribute huge amounts to the geologic knowledge of the country. In 1836, Eaton created a floating museum/school on the Erie Canal, where students explored natural history on their way to Lake Erie and back. This trip would have a tremendous impact on many future scientists.

In fact, the geological profession calls the period 1818–1836 the "Eatonian Era" in honor of the success of Eaton's promotion of geology during that time. By 1860, seven graduates of Eaton were in charge of geological surveys throughout the country, a feat unmatched by any university to this day.

Many of Eaton's students went on to build their own reputations and fame in the field. Eaton's influence on the following people, and their subsequent contributions, has never been equaled. The following set of short biographies are just a sample of some of Eaton's mentoring successes.

Stephen Van Rensselaer loaned Amos Eaton $300 to start the Rensselaer School, now Rensselaer Polytechnic Institute, more than 175 years ago.

Amos Eaton is known as the father of American geology. No other scientist/ teacher has made such an impact on the discipline.

Joseph Henry (1797–1878), one of the students on Eaton's flotilla down the Erie Canal, became the first director of the Smithsonian Institution (1846). Henry was born across the river in Albany in 1797 and lived at 105 Columbia Street, not far from City Hall. Henry was the inventor of the electric motor and is called the father of daily weather forecasts. (He established 600 observation stations around the country in two years.)

Henry taught at the Boys Academy next to his home and discovered a way to transmit sound over wire by magnetic force (the telegraph) in 1832. He was a friend of S.F.B. Morse, who went on to perfect the Morse code, and also a big supporter of Alexander Graham Bell in his invention of the telephone.

Henry was a founding member of the American Association for the Advancement of Science (AAAS) in 1848, and later its president. The AAAS was the first permanent organization formed to promote the development of science and engineering at the national level representing all disciplines. Joseph Henry was also one of the original members of a group that later became the National Academy of Sciences in 1863, and served as its second president.

When Henry died on May 16, 1878, the entire federal government closed. His funeral was attended by the president, vice-president, cabinet, Supreme Court judges, members of Congress, and others. Henry was one of the most respected scientists in the country.

James Eights (1798–1882) was another of Eaton's students and a member of the Erie Canal flotilla. In fact, Eights produced a number of maps and etchings of the canal trip that have been widely reproduced around the world. Eights was born on North Pearl Street in Albany and was an Albany physician but never practiced medicine. Instead, he became the first American naturalist to visit and study the Antarctic on a quasi-government–backed expedition organized by Edmund Fanning. This "Voyage of Discovery" sailed from Connecticut ports for the South Seas in October 1829. Eights wrote the first geological and botanical description of parts of the Antarctic area. He explored Patagonia, Deception and Staaten Islands, Tierra del Fuego, and the South Shetland Islands. He also discovered three new species of crustacea and won scientific praise.

Locally, Eights painted early Albany street scenes, but it is his geological work that is praised in scientific circles. Eights was later appointed to go on the first government-sanctioned Wilkes Expedition back to Antarctica in 1838, but was bumped. He spent the rest of his life writing and popularizing science in local magazines and journals. He briefly left the area and was a geologist in North Carolina in the 1850s, but his major contribution, which is still praised, is his work in the Antarctic.

Joseph Henry, the Albany-born student of Eaton, became the first director of the Smithsonian Institute.

His work in describing the natural history of the Albany Pine Bush in 1836 in *Every Day Naturalist Book* was instrumental in showing the negative impact that development has had on the region today. Eights died in 1882 at the age of 84 in Ballston Spa.

James Hall (1811–1898) was known as the father of the geosyncline, a geological concept that lasted 100 years (and not even mentioned in textbooks now). Hall was appointed New York State's state geologist in 1836 and is considered today to be the "Father of American Paleontology." Hall received two degrees from Rensselaer and became a professor at the school (1835–1841), which still holds his paleontological collections.

The 1856 annual meeting of the American Association for the Advancement of Science was held in Albany and was organized by Hall, who was also the AAAS president. The meeting involved the dedication of two major scientific facilities in Albany: the New York State Geological Museum (now the New York State Museum) and the Dudley Observatory, both still in existence. Hall also presented his famous paper on the theory of "geosynclines."

James Eights, another Albany-born Eaton student, illustrated much of the geology on the Erie Canal in 1828.

Lewis C. Beck, from nearby Schenectady, was also a medical doctor and was appointed the first junior professor at RPI under Eaton. In 1829, he became New York's state mineralogist. That year, his brother T. Romeyn Beck and Governor William L. Marcy (another Troy native) appointed Beck to survey the state's mineral resources. By 1842, he had traveled over 8,000 miles and published one of the classics of the state's geological survey.

Fay Edgerton (1803–1832) was 21 years old when he entered the Rensselaer School, and in 1826, he became Eaton's adjunct, a position he held until he graduated in 1828. He went on to become a professor of natural history at the Utica Gymnasium in Utica, New York. It was there that he had James Dana as a student and encouraged him to go into natural history, which Dana did at the Rensselaer School. He became one of Eaton's best students.

Ebenezer Emmons Sr. (1800–1863) became a junior professor at Rensselaer in 1830 and stayed there for ten years. He became the state geologist for the northern New York State district in 1836. Emmons is the person who named the Adirondacks (1838) and Taconic Mountains (1844). He later became the state geologist for North Carolina, and throughout his career, published several classic geology texts in 1826, 1842, 1854, and 1860.

James C. Booth (1810–1888) was appointed assistant to the First Geologic Survey of Pennsylvania, conducted by Henry Darwin Rogers, a 26-year-old professor at the University of Pennsylvania, in 1836. A native Philadelphian, Booth studied with William H. Keating at the University of Pennsylvania and with Eaton. He studied chemistry for three years in Germany and Austria. After that, he established a laboratory in Philadelphia for instruction in chemical analysis and application of chemistry to the arts. It was the first of its kind in the country.

Booth published on the geological survey of the state of Delaware, including the application of the geological observations to agriculture during the 1830s. Booth was appointed state geologist in the spring of 1837 and was given a salary of $1,000 per year for two years, and no funds for assistants. Regardless, he traveled the state for two years recording his observations and paying special attention to those areas deemed best for agriculture. Only 200 copies of his report, *Memoir of the Geological Survey of the State of Delaware: including the application of the Geological Observations to Agriculture*, were published in 1844.

In 1852, Booth published *The Encyclopedia of Chemistry, Practical and Theoretical Embracing Its Application to the Arts, Metallurgy, Mineralogy, Geology, Medicine, and Pharmacy* along with Campbell Morfit. The 4,974-page book was published in Philadelphia by H.C. Baird. Booth also participated in the Pacific Railroad Surveys (1853), and was later appointed melter and refiner at the Philadelphia mint, where he introduced the term "nickel" into American currency.

James D. Dana (1813–1895) was a member of the U.S. expedition to the Pacific and Antarctic (1838–1842) under Charles Wilkes, trips that formed the basis for much of his later writing on zoology and mineralogy. With his father-in-law, Benjamin Silliman, he edited the *American Journal of Science* (1846–1895). His writings include manuals of geology and mineralogy, two treatises on corals, and a text on Hawaiian volcanoes; he is considered by some as America's first volcanologist.

In 1888, James D. Dana, along with James Hall and Alexander Winchell, founded the Geological Society of America in New York, the first enduring society for the geosciences in America. Dana's *A System of Mineralogy*, published in 1837, is a compilation of all minerals outside Europe. He published the *Manual of Mineralogy* in 1848, and it is still being printed. A monument dedicated to Dana is located on Madison Avenue in Albany.

Asa Fitch (1803–1879) became the first New York State entomologist in 1845. He studied the effects of noxious insects on agriculture, and his publications became the standard for showing how science can solve public issues. Fitch published some 103 papers and addresses during his 17 years as state entomologist, gaining international fame as an economic and systematic entomologist. He described a large number of the most important insect pests and parasites in the country. Fitch also became a noted historian, writing several volumes about his hometown of Salem and extensively about Eaton's Erie Canal trips.

George H. Cook (1818–1889) wrote the *Geology of New Jersey* in 1868 but is credited with helping to create Rutgers University as a land-grant institution earlier in 1864. Cook became the first non-clerical–trained, full-time faculty member at Rutgers. He made a critical difference in the fight with Princeton for land-grant designation since he knew the state better than anyone at Princeton due to his experience as assistant state geologist. Both he and David Murry, a professor of mathematics, successfully lobbied the legislature. Later, Cook established the Agricultural Experiment Station on the College Farm. He is considered the most important single figure at nineteenth-century Rutgers.

Ezra Slocum Carr (1819–1894) was born in Stephentown, Rensselaer County, on March 9, 1819. He graduated from Vermont's Castleton Medical College in 1842, with a medical degree, taking the chair of chemistry and natural history in that institution immediately. He was also a lecturer in medical schools in Philadelphia, and at one time served in the Vermont Legislature. In 1856, he arrived at Wisconsin University and served for 12 years as professor of chemistry and natural history, as well as a commissioner of the state geological survey and a member of the board of regents (1857–1859). In 1869, he became a professor at the University of California, a position he held for six years, and later served as state superintendent of public instruction.

According to Kevin Starr's book *Inventing the Dream*, beginning in 1876, Ezra S. Carr and his wife, Jeanne, made a special project of developing the gardens of their Pasadena estate, Carmelita, which eventually became a public park. It helped "establish a lavish landscaping tradition which made Pasadena the premier garden and floral city of Southern California."

Douglass Houghton (1809–1845), who was born in Troy, is said to have been one of Eaton's brightest students, graduating in 1829. In 1829–1830, he was assistant professor of chemistry and natural history at the Rensselaer School. In 1842–1843, he was elected mayor of Detroit, Michigan.

Houghton prepared the geological survey of Michigan and convinced Congress to conduct a complete geological survey of the western United States, which he began in 1844. Houghton and four others drowned on Lake Superior in 1845 and never completed the study.

James Hall, known as the father of American paleontology, was also a student of Eaton. Hall's long career made a lasting impact on geology.

Eben Horsford (1818–1893) was a civil engineering student and was intrigued by the chemistry of bread and efforts to replace yeast as a leavening agent. He produced a blend of calcium acid phosphate and sodium bicarbonate, making the first commercial baking powder. It is still being made today by Rumford Baking Powder, a company that Horsford started with George F. Wilson. Horsford also participated in the Pacific Railroad Surveys (1853). After two years at Justus Liebig's laboratory at Giessen, Germany, he was elected to the Rumford Professorship at Harvard, where he helped form the Lawrence Scientific School and developed the first U.S. laboratory for teaching analytical chemistry.

All of these men had the great fortune of being taught by Amos Eaton.

Amos Eaton and Stephen Van Rensselaer's vision of their school continued as it became a science center throughout the nineteenth century and produced many leading scientists and engineers. Rensselaer Polytechnic Institute (RPI) was founded as the Rensselaer School in 1824 "for the purpose of instructing persons . . . in the application of science to the common purposes of life," as stated in a letter from Stephen Van Rensselaer to Samuel Blatchford on November 5, 1824. His complete letter to the Reverend Dr. Blatchford, first president of the school, explained further his purpose. It read as follows:

Dear Sir

I have established a school at the north end of Troy, in Rensselaer County in the building usually called the Old Bank Place, for the purpose of instructing persons, who may choose to apply themselves, in the application of science to the common purposes of life. My principal object is, to qualify teachers for instructing the sons and daughters of farmers and mechanics, by lectures or otherwise, in the application of experimental chemistry, philosophy and natural history, to agriculture, domestic economy, the arts and manufactures. From the trials which have been made by persons in my employment at Utica, Whitesborough, Rome, Auburn, and Geneva, during the last summer, I am inclined to believe that competent instructors may be produced in the school at Troy, who will be highly useful to the community in the diffusion of a very useful kind of knowledge, with its application to the business of living.

The original school was located in the former Farmer's Bank on the corner of Middleburgh and River Streets.

Eaton tried to provide education for women, offering a "ladies course," as early as 1824 to fulfill this original mission. A room was even fitted, according to a letter that he wrote to Emma Willard:

Mrs Willard,

I have given the regular notice to S. Blatchford, Prest. of the Rensselaer School, that it is in readiness. He and several of the other officers have inspected the rooms, apparatus, &c. and pronounced all compleat. This will soon be published. The object of this note is, to request you to visit the place, and examine my plan of arrangement. Perhaps one of your tutoresses may attend, and become a practical or operative chemist, so as to be able to give instruction at home. There will be one section of young ladies, I think. For this course, no fees [will] be charged to Ladies, who are preparing for giving instruction in chemistry. Will you honour me with a call tomorrow?

Yours respectfully,
Amos Eaton
Dec. 24th 1824.

In 1835, he did enroll a class of eight young women in a special mathematics course to prove that women could learn the same as men. When he requested the school's board to "test" the women after the completion of the course in February 1835, they agreed that Eaton had succeeded, but did not embrace the continuation of women at the school.

To the board of Examiners for Rensselaer Institute
February 11th 1835.

A class of eight young ladies have received instruction here for the period of one quarter in practical mathematics, by way of experiments.—To wit, S.A.M. Aikin, Eliza Eddy, S.C. Eaton, Laura Johnson, L.A. Palmer, F.E. Tuttle, Juliette Wallace, Abbey H. Lindlay.

We do not offer them for a formal examination, as this is not authorized by precedent. On our own account we respectfully ask, that you will question some of them, so far as to be enabled to draw a fair comparison, between the study of speculative geometry and algebra as generally practiced in female seminaries, and this mode of applying mathematics, to the essential calculations of Geography, Astronomy, Meteorology, necessary measurements &c.

Amos Eaton, Sen. Prof.
T.R. Hopkins, Adj. Prof.

The original Rensselaer School was the former Farmer's Bank on the corner of Middleburgh and River Streets.

RPI moved into new quarters on Eighth Street above Seventh Street. It burned in 1904 and was replaced with the Approach, a classical staircase link between the city and school.

However, those eight women did go on to Emma Willard's Troy Female Seminary. Eaton did not give up his quest for teaching women. He took charge of the new science department and taught science to the female students at the seminary.

In 1833, Eaton's school became the Rensselaer Institute. In the 1850s, its scope was broadened, turning it into a polytechnic institution, and in 1861, the name was changed to the present Rensselaer Polytechnic Institute. Eaton, who was sick most of his adult life, never stopped his dedication to teaching, and he spent the rest of his life at the school in some capacity.

In a letter written on April 1, 1824, to his son Amos B. Eaton, Eaton tried to instill the virtues of being focused on work and study. He gave his son several principles to live by:

> 1. I never studied late in the evening.
>
> 2d. When I felt the least degree of giddiness, I stopped my studies instantly for an hour or two, however I might be occupied. I would then walk about or converse with idlers.
>
> 3d. I drank no ardent spirit, nor wine, cider, nor strong beer for ten or fifteen years. Nor to this day, excepting beer.
>
> 4th. I always made it a practice to eat considerably. I do not believe in starving students; though I would not make gormandizers of them.
>
> 5th. I never leaned forward in studying or writing. It is perfectly easy to acquire a habit of sitting up, so as to keep the breast strait [*sic*]. And I had always a high desk to stand by part of the time.

6th. Whether sitting or standing, I always varied my position perpetually. This I found to be very important to health, besides keeping the mind more active. No evil arose from it, excepting a little scolding from [your] grandmother Eaton, about my coat sleeves and the seat of my pantaloons.

7th. When my mind was confused with a subject of study, I always left it for a little jolly conversation an hour, and then resumed it with a clear head.

NINETEENTH-CENTURY SCIENTIFIC POWERHOUSE

Eaton's Rensselaer School, now Rensselaer Polytechnic Institute, produced many leading scientists and engineers during the nineteenth century and later. The following names are just a sample of these, in addition to those names already mentioned earlier in the chapter.

Leffert L. Buck (1837–1909) built and restored bridges and was the builder of the longest bridge in the world in 1903—the Williamsburg Bridge across the East River in New York City—and then, the highest bridge in the world in Peru in the 1870s.

Alexander J. Cassatt (1839–1906) became president of the Pennsylvania Railroad in 1899 and introduced many improvements in the railroad industry. He is responsible for the construction of the Pennsylvania terminal in Manhattan, which required tunneling under the Hudson River.

Sanford Cluett (1874–1968), who was head of Troy's Cluett, Peabody & Company's manufacturing and research, held more than 200 patents including a process named for him, "Sanforizing," which helps reduce shrinkage in fabrics.

William B. Cogswell (1834–1921) is credited with founding the alkali industry in America, and his company, the Solvay Process Company, became the largest maker of soda ash and byproducts in the country.

Mordecai T. Endicott (1844–1926) was given control of all civil engineering projects in the U.S. Navy by 1890. He is called the "Father of the Civil Engineering Corps" and was appointed chief of the Bureau of Yards and Docks by President William Mckinley, a post always before held by the office of the line.

George W.G. Ferris (1859–1896) designed the original Ferris Wheel for Chicago's World Columbian Exposition in 1893. It stood 250 feet high.

William Gurley (1821–1887) was an early manufacturer of precision instruments such as transits. Gurley's instruments are world renowned for quality.

Alexander Holley (1832–1882), called the father of the modern American steel industry, introduced the Bessemer steel process into America at Troy in the 1860s, and worked with John Winslow.

Emil H. Praeger (1882–1973) designed New York's Tappan Zee Bridge and a portable harbor for Allied troops during the invasion of Normandy, and played key roles in the renovation of the White House.

Washington A. Roebling (1837–1926), along with his wife, Emily Warren Roebling (1844–1903), are famous for building the Brooklyn Bridge.

Henry A. Rowland (1848–1901), called the foremost scientist America had yet produced in 1924 by the president of the American Academy of Sciences, invented concave spectral grating, which helped revise the solar spectrum and many measuring devices.

Built in 1856 as a Methodist college, Troy University didn't last long and its building went through a variety of uses. The structure was commonly called the "Towers of Troy" since its spires could be seen everywhere.

James H. Salisbury (1823–1905) was a doctor and nutritionist, and the "Salisbury Steak" was named for him.

John L. Riddell (1807–1865) invented the binocular microscope and magnifying glass.

Edwin Thacher (1839–1920) introduced a special type of cylindrical slide rule that was popular.

John F. Winslow (1810–1892) helped to build the ironclad USS *Monitor* as owner of the Rensselaer Iron Works and the Corning Iron Works, both located in Troy, New York. Along with Alexander Holly, he purchased the rights to manufacture and sell Bessemer steel in 1864. He became the fifth president of RPI in 1865.

EARLY PALEONTOLOGY

Silas Watson Ford, a Troy telegrapher and an amateur paleontologist, made some of the most important discoveries regarding Cambrian paleontology in the nineteenth century. He found the first early Cambrian period fossils in North America, helping to resolve a geological controversy that had been going on for 30 years.

In his short life span, Ford published more than 23 scientific papers. His seven-part series of geological processes in the *New York Tribune* in 1879 was so popular that Union College awarded him an honorary master's degree.

The Ford family was originally from Glenville. Silas and his family moved to Schenectady after the death of his parents, and then to Troy. His brother Stephen Van Rensselaer Ford went from being a station agent for the Rensselaer and Saratoga Railroad in 1854 to a joint partnership with George P. Ide in 1865 to make collars and cuffs. Ide & Ford located their business at 506 Fulton Street.

Silas Ford appears to have moved to Troy the following year, boarding at 208 North Second Street, and was listed as a telegraph operator. His brother Isaac was a telegraph operator at the Union Railroad depot and Isaac probably trained his younger brother. Later, Silas is listed as a bookkeeper and may have worked at Stephen's collar company. The partnership dissolved between Ford and Ide, and George Ide went on to become one of Troy's largest collar companies. Silas went back to work as a telegraph operator, but his keen interest in geology finally led him to James Hall, the state geologist in Albany.

Hall and fellow geologist Ebenezer Emmons were in an intellectual battle at the time. Emmons had proposed the Taconic System to describe the formation of the Taconic Mountains and rocks of easternmost New York and western Massachusetts. Emmons had given an older Cambrian age (540 to 505 million years ago) to these rocks while Hall said they were younger, of Ordovician age (500 to 438 million years ago).

The Taconic Orogeny or mountain-building period happened about 450 million years ago when a volcanic island arc collided with proto-North America (around the Connecticut Valley region). This event ran from Newfoundland to Alabama. The rocks, which had originally been deposited in a deep-water area, were stacked together by these plate collisions and formed the Taconic Mountain range. Originally, this mountain range was as high as the Himalayas, but it quickly eroded and the sediments were deposited into a shallow sea that covered most of the middle half of proto-North America.

In Troy, one can see this overthrust where older rocks are sitting on top of younger rocks (especially in the Mount Ida Gorge), and geologists attempted to explain this anomaly (now called the Emmons Thrust, earlier Logan's Fault). Ford had found fossils in parts of these rocks in Beman Park that helped to explain the older age of the rocks and in the long run helped support Emmons's theories. Eventually, Emmons was proven correct. Emmons is buried close to Hall in Albany Rural Cemetery, and it is reported that he is facing Hall in his grave.

Ford jumped into the fray. His discoveries of fossils of Cambrian age proved that portions of the Taconic were older than Hall had proposed. While not formally trained in geology, early on he wrote to Hall, at the urging of William Gurley, a Troy industrialist (Gurley made scientific instruments such as the transit), in an attempt to get help and guidance in training in geology, his real passion. Ford had offered loans of his fossils to Hall, and Hall visited Ford in Troy.

In 1871, Ford published an important article in the *American Journal of Science* that correlated the Troy rocks to the older Cambrian period and described the first ever fossil, *Hyolithes opercula*, found in North America. This established Ford, at age 23, as a leading authority on Cambrian fauna east of the Hudson. He even had one of his fossils named after him by a leading paleontologist in 1881. *Fordilla troyensis* is one of the oldest known bivalves in the world.

Throughout all of this, Ford was still a telegraph operator, though working for the American Telegraph Company, then absorbed into Western Union, at 249 River Street, where City Hall is today.

What appeared to be a promising career, however, came to an early end. Ford temporarily worked with the U.S. Geological Survey, got married, and was prolific in his writings. But Ford had either an alcohol or opium addiction and always seemed to be in debt, constantly needing to borrow money. Eventually, most of the geologists with whom he had been corresponding or working wrote him off. Ford had a $72.20 debt that he couldn't afford to pay.

Separated from her husband, Ford's wife tried to sell off his fossil collection of 419 specimens and a 170-volume personal library to repay the debt. Ford himself had been declared legally incompetent, so Mrs. Ford assumed all liability for the debt. James Hall tried to get the State Regents to buy the fossil collection, but problems arose and continued to occur when they agreed to buy it then reneged on the deal. While the state bickered back and forth, Mrs. Ford died on February 24, 1895. The collection was finally purchased (no one knows who the seller was) in 1900 for $70.70 and is now in the state paleontology collections. No one knows what happened to Ford's personal library, but it may have been lost in the great capitol fire of 1911, in which almost half a million of the state's library collections were lost.

Four months after Mrs. Ford died, Silas, at age 47, died at his cousin's home in Wilton on June 25, 1895, and was buried in Schenectady's Vale Cemetery.

THE OIL MAN

The name Powers is well known in Lansingburgh, now part of Troy. William Powers, a former schoolteacher, started a successful oil cloth factory on Second Avenue in 1817. After a freak accident took his life, his wife, Deborah, and two sons, Albert and Nathaniel, carried on the business. They became one of the leading business families in the village, operating a bank and opera house and helping to fund schools and the needy.

In 1862, Albert had a son, A.W. In 1884, at the age of 22, A.W. married Matilda Wheeler Page, and they had one son, Sidney, who was born in 1890. Sidney Powers is one of the most respected names in American geology today. Powers attended school in Troy, and at the age of 21, he earned his bachelor's degree in geology from nearby Williams College.

Powers's early work in Oklahoma was a major event in the evolution of the field of petroleum geology and the oil industry. At the time, most oil searching was done by looking at hills and valleys, mostly a surficial geology approach. Powers promoted the importance of looking underground instead, and this led to the beginning of the use of drill cuttings and geophysical prospecting, according to Dr. Gerald Friedman of the Northeastern Science Foundation.

During his short lifetime, Powers published 124 articles that explained how to use geology to find oil, and his writings are still used around the world. Powers was a founding father of the American Association of Petroleum Geologists (AAPG), today the largest geological society in the world. In fact, "the Sidney Power Medal" is the AAPG's most prestigious honor. Powers died in 1932 and is buried at Oakwood Cemetery.

Emma Willard began her school for women in Troy in 1821.

TROY'S HART SISTERS

Emma Hart Willard and Almira Hart Lincoln Phelps are two names associated with Troy but admired in education circles throughout the country. In 1807, Emma Hart (1787–1870), a young Connecticut woman and the next-to-last of 17 children, began her lifelong work to bring women equal access to education. This was a time in history when women were not allowed in college, but rather were confined to female academies that specialized in classes "suitable" for girls.

Her success in teaching in Connecticut prompted her to write *An Address to the Public; Particularly to the Members of the Legislature of New York, Proposing a Plan for Improving Female Education* in 1819. The New York legislature did not do anything (some members even thought she was crazy), but the pamphlet was noticed by both Thomas Jefferson and John Adams.

Also impressed was Governor DeWitt Clinton, who invited Willard to open a school in New York State. In 1819, she opened a school in Waterford. However, several of Troy's visionaries convinced the city fathers to raise $4,000 in taxes to begin construction of a school for Willard. They purchased the old coffee house next to the village green between Second, First, and Congress and began renovations. Willard and company moved into the "Troy Female Seminary" in 1821, and today the school continues its mission in Troy, over 180 years later. Like many other leaders impressed with her work, the Marquis de Lafayette visited Troy twice during his American tours in 1824 and 1825, and both times visited with Willard.

According to one history, the seminary was the first such school, predating the first public high schools for girls in Boston and New York City by 5 years and the famous Mary Lyon's Mount Holyoke Seminary by 16 years. The seminary was a pioneer in the teaching of science, mathematics, and social studies, and attracted students from wealthy families. By 1831, there was an enrollment of more than 300 students, with more than 100 boarding at the school.

However, one of the biggest problems in female education was finding suitable textbooks. All textbooks at the time were written for men. So, Emma wrote some of the school's textbooks: *History of the United States, or Republic of America* (1828), *A System of Universal History in Perspective* (1835), as well as a volume of poetry, *The Fulfillment of a Promise* (1831).

Emma Willard headed the college until 1838, by which time she had helped shape the future of hundreds of women. She continued to lecture and write, including *A Treatise on the Motive Powers Which Produce the Circulation of the Blood* (1846); *Guide to the Temple of Time, Universal History for Schools*, and *Last Leaves of American History* (1849); *Astronography, or Astronomical Geography* (1854); and *Morals for the Young* (1857). She died in Troy in 1870, and the school was renamed for her in 1895. It moved to its present location in 1910.

Emma's youngest sister, Almira Hart, also made an impact on female education. She followed in Emma's footsteps in her formative years, teaching at Berlin Academy, and in 1817, she married Simeon Lincoln, editor of the Hartford's *Connecticut Mirror*. His death only six years later brought Almira to Troy to teach in her sister's Troy Female Seminary.

Emma Willard's sister Almira helped Emma at her school and later became famous for writing textbooks for girls.

The Emma Willard School still operates on a campus built in 1910 off Pawling Avenue.

While in Troy, two people had a great influence on her—her sister Emma and Amos Eaton, the founder of RPI. Eaton introduced her to new methods of teaching called the Pestalozzi method, based on the methods of Swiss education reformer Johann Heinrich Pestalozzi (1746–1827), who advocated educating the poor. This system emphasized two teaching methods: instructors should start with the simple and proceed to the complicated, and teachers should provide a "hands-on" lecture. Most of these principles are used in modern elementary education.

Almira implemented both methods in her classrooms in Troy. Almira taught and served as principal at Troy for eight years. During that time, she began writing textbooks, like her sister, on botany, natural philosophy (physics), geology, and, specifically, chemistry. Some of her popular works were *Familiar Lectures on Botany* (1829), *Dictionary of Chemistry* (1830), *Botany for Beginners* (1833), *Chemistry for Beginners* (1834), and *Familiar Lectures on Chemistry* (1838). Her textbooks were used throughout the United States. In 1859, Almira became the second woman ever elected into the American Association for the Advancement of Science.

RUSSELL SAGE COLLEGE

Russell Sage (1816–1906), who has a leading women's college in his name, was born in Oneida County in 1816. He was engaged in the grocery business in Troy and became quite successful. In 1841, he was first elected as an alderman of the city and then reelected until 1848. For seven years, he was the treasurer of Rensselaer County (1844–1851) and was elected to Congress as a Whig; he served two terms there, from 1853 to 1857.

Sage became wealthy from banking and railroad stocks after moving to New York City in 1863. Along with Jay Gould, he took financial control of several Western railroads, as well as the elevated railway system in New York City and the Western Union Telegraph Company. An assassin, Henry Norcross, tried to kill him in 1891 but failed.

In 1906, Sage died on Long Island and left his entire fortune of about $70 million to his wife, Margaret Olivia Slocum Sage (1828–1918). Mr. Sage was buried nearby at Oakwood Cemetery. Historians through the ages have inferred Sage's dislike of women, so it is ironic that in 1916, his wife founded Russell Sage College, an all-girls school in Troy. The Russell Sage campus is located on the campus of the old Emma Willard School. Mrs. Sage also donated large sums of money to the Emma Willard School and to RPI. The college continues to teach women.

In 1907, Mrs. Sage established the Russell Sage Foundation with an endowment of $15 million to work on social issues. In 1912, she also purchased Marsh Island in the Gulf of Mexico and gave it to the State of Louisiana as a bird sanctuary.

Mrs. Russell Sage purchased the former Emma Willard School on Second Street and turned it into the Russell Sage College for Women.

9. THE RISE OF THE IRON INDUSTRY

The iron and steel industries helped make Troy a leading manufacturing center during the nineteenth century. However, to understand how that happened, one must become familiar with the evolution of the iron industry as a whole in America and New York State, in particular.

The iron industry in New York State, and particularly in the Hudson Valley region, developed at a much slower rate than it had in the rest of the early American colonies during the seventeenth and eighteenth centuries. By 1700, ironworks had been established in Massachusetts, Pennsylvania, Maryland, Virginia, New Jersey, and Delaware, but not in New York.

The early Dutch inhabitants of New York knew that iron ore, forests for charcoal, and limestone for fluxing were available in sufficient quantities for iron production as early as 1656, yet it was not until 96 years after the first blast furnace at Saugus, Massachusetts (1646–1668), that New York produced its own pig iron. Once started, however, New York became the second-largest producer of pig iron in the country by 1810. New York's iron industry began in the Hudson Valley, and it was here and in the northern Adirondack region that the state's iron industry firmly settled.

Why did it take longer for New York to begin an iron industry, particularly when New York was one of the first settled states? What factors led to New York's sudden rise in iron production after the American Revolution and into the nineteenth century? Did New York's iron industry reflect national trends during the nineteenth century?

Perhaps the commercial success of early Dutch and English traders in the fur trade during the seventeenth and eighteenth centuries precluded the development of an iron industry. In fact, those in power during the seventeenth century purposely discouraged iron production for fear of takeover by neighboring colonies.

New York's slow population growth was due in part to this effort to prevent competition to the fur trade by newcomers and by a legitimate fear of French and Indian attacks. Moreover, the feudal-like, manorial land system that developed after 1680 controlled the populated areas of the state and the resulting leasehold system confined tenants to an agrarian mode of existence for nearly 150 years.

Since iron making was both labor and capital intensive, it prohibited tenants on manor lands from engaging in the business. Additionally, the apparent lack of interest by the majority of landholders (except, somewhat, Philip Livingston and Henry Beekman), who had the capital and labor force, was a major force in shaping what industries would develop in the Hudson Valley region.

The full development of New York's industry did not take place with the Dutch or English mainstream population, but rather with the Yankee (New England) population invasion of the 1790s and the breakdown of the leasehold system. This was followed by the utilization of abundant iron ores in the Hudson Highlands region, which were successfully exploited by non-manorial freemen backed by capital of New York City origin, and followed by the discovery of major iron ore deposits in the Adirondack region at the beginning of the nineteenth century.

The building of the Champlain, Erie, and Delaware and Hudson Canals during the first quarter of the nineteenth century allowed easy access and transit of raw and finished products. These factors, combined with the discovery and utilization of the finest molding sand in the Hudson Valley, led to the industry's centralization in this region. By 1860, New York and the Hudson Valley were producing 75,000 tons of pig iron, ranking it third in the country.

THE HUDSON VALLEY DURING THE SEVENTEENTH CENTURY

The founding of both New Amsterdam (Manhattan) and Fort Orange (Albany) during the early seventeenth century by the Dutch West India Company was a commercial venture in the truest sense. The preamble of the company's 1621 charter stated that the company's aim was to maintain trade and navigation for the prosperity of the mother country. By the 1630s, the Dutch had extended their fur-trading grasp along the 150-mile Hudson River corridor (Manhattan to Albany) and 30 to 40 miles along the Raritan and Delaware Rivers. This territory was sparsely settled up until 1664; the Dutch population was centered in New York, Kingston, and Albany. Yet, by the 1650s, more than 34,000 beaver pelts were exported from Albany and its vicinity, signifying the fervor at which the Dutch were trading. While much of the Hudson Highlands was unsettled during this period because the land was "not improvable by human industry," 100 years later, this area would become the center of New York's iron industry.

Fur trading was a monopoly enjoyed by the Dutch West India Company. In fact, the slowness of New York's population growth is attributed to the company's unwillingness to import people for fear of undue competition for pelts, and it was not until the company suffered continuous deficits that it attempted to colonize its lands in 1629 and 1640. The company extended offers of huge land grants and privileges to any stockholder of the company who would plant a colony of 50 or more families, creating the famous patroonship system.

As mentioned in previous chapters, Kiliaen Van Rensselaer, a merchant and stockholder, was the first to take the offer and establish a colony around Fort Orange, which he populated with Walloons (from the southern portion of Belgium) in 1630. Several other patroonships followed, but they were not an immediate success. The company, still fearing competition, did little to encourage further colonization. Also, the patroons found it difficult to entice settlers to submit to a feudal-like system, especially when there was

Hundreds of canal boats wait to enter the Watervliet Side Cut opposite Troy's Broadway.

abundant free land available in the New Netherlands and surrounding colonies. The Colony of Rensselaerwyck succeeded for the most part because Rensselaer paid the majority of costs associated with settlement.

The profits of the fur trade were enjoyed both by the company and the settlers of Rensselaerwyck, leading to many conflicts between the two groups. This competition for furs was a natural extension of the Dutch ethic. Unlike their English counterparts, the social status of the Dutch was based on a mercantilistic basis, not the landed estates characteristic of the English. The Dutch were merchants by class, and competition with the French to the north and English to the east was a natural extension from home. It was imperative to them to control the trade at Albany and ensure the uninterrupted flow of furs to New York and the mother country. This led to an effort by traders of Albany to discourage settlement west of there by anyone. Native American troubles in 1643–1644 and 1658–1664 and problems with the French and Indian allies also discouraged settlement in outlying areas. The burning of Schenectady by the French in 1690 was a direct result of the French wanting control of the Hudson River—and therefore, control of the North American fur trade.

The takeover of New Netherland by the English in 1664 did not immediately change the slow growth in population of New York. From 1664 to 1678, the population only grew by 2,000, which is estimated by one historian to barely accommodate the natural rise by births. Moreover, Sir Edmund Andros, then governor, even through promotional activities, estimated that only 20,000 acres in New York were newly taken up and patented in 1678. Immigration from Holland understandably declined after the British takeover, although trade continued for a short time. These factors, combined with the fear of natives and a perception that the land east and west of the Highlands and Taconics offered little, painted a bleak picture of New York. So bleak that the governors of New York wanted to annex neighboring colonies to make up for New York's supposed lack of resources.

The Griswold Wire Works was one of many industries along the Poestenkill.

The development of large manorial and non-manorial patents in the late seventeenth and eighteenth centuries did increase the population of New York. More than 30 manorial and non-manorial patents were created in the Hudson Valley, comprising some 2 million acres of land—the development of which was dependent on labor by agriculturally based tenant farming. The leasing of these lands by way of a feudal-like obligation of various forms of tenure ensured the wealth of the landlords. Resentment, however, on the part of the tenants over economic and political constraints made the Hudson Valley a boiling pot for many years, leading to the so-called Anti-Rent controversies between 1750 and 1840. The insecurities faced by many of the tenants over the tenure system, the shift from a self-sufficient to a market-dependent agrarian economy, and the lack of large sums of capital all but precluded the development of an iron industry by tenants on manorial lands. Moreover, it was quite evident in many of the tenants' leases, as shown by a lease to Cornelius Brusie on the Livingston Patent, that they did not have possession of the following:

> All stream, creeks, runs of water, and all mines, minerals and oars with power
> to erect mills, dams, and other erections and buildings, proper for stamping,
> melting or otherwise manufacturing and preserving the oar within the demised
> premises together with timber, firewood, stone, and all other materials, to
> be found . . . that may be useful for the purposes aforesaid, or for any other use
> . . . whatsoever.

THE BEGINNINGS OF NEW YORK'S IRON INDUSTRY

In 1737, Governor George Clark, aware of New York's lack of an iron industry and growth of surrounding colonies, addressed the 11th session of the 20th Assembly and stated the following:

> I recommended to you the last session to find some proper encouragement for raising of hemp, and promoting of ship building; I now add to them that of iron. They are things that deserve utmost attention and call for a speedy help.

Clark's concern was warranted, as all the iron used by New Yorkers came either from England or the surrounding colonies. Between 1710 and 1735, 1,545 tons of wrought iron and 1,206 tons of bar iron were imported from England.

There is some evidence that an ironworks commenced shortly after Clark's address on the Cortland Manor. In 1745, Henry Beekman, who owned the Rhinebeck, Beekman, and later the Cortland and part of the Rumbout Patent via the marriage of Gertrude Van Cortlandt, advertised as available for leasing "a fine furnace all fitted for blasting" with "four large beds of good iron ore within two miles of the furnace." He further stated that the works had been built and run by one Ephraim Hayward and Company since the late 1730s.

While it appears that Beekman was not interested in the iron industry himself, his neighbor and fellow landowner Robert Livingston, second Lord of the Manor, was keenly interested in the establishment of what was perhaps the first ironworks in New York State. Livingston erected an ironworks consisting of a furnace and forge on the Ancram or Roeloff Jansen's Kill, about 14 miles from the Hudson at an initial cost of 6,000 pounds. Ore for the works was brought by cart through the woods from an "ore hill" in Salisbury, Connecticut, 12 miles from the works. Even though Livingston owned part of this mine, the hauling of the ore proved expensive. To complicate matters, the resulting iron had to be hauled to the Hudson for eventual shipping to New York City markets.

The expense in hauling ore was only one problem encountered by the Livingston family. The running of ironworks like Ancram required from 60 to 100 men, including colliers (charcoal makers) and teamsters. While some of these workers were Livingston's tenants, a labor shortage arose early in the operation. Livingston wrote to John Dewitt in January 1741, "about the ironworks, I wish we could get 24 or 30 hands employed to cut wood and 6 to 8 good honest colliers."

Keeping his ironworks in mind, Livingston again wrote to Dewitt two months later about the arrival of 17 Highland Scottish families and wanted them placed on "a tract as conveniently near ancram as may be that they may make money of ye wood which they must otherwise destroy and burn for nothing." He went on to say that if they did well, it would encourage others to settle by them, but he was disappointed that "there be no colliers among the highlanders but some tolerable ax men."

The Ancram ironworks produced over 3,300 tons of pig iron between 1750 and 1756, an average of 500 tons a year; some 65 tons were made into castings. Yet, during this period, Robert Livingston had some major problems at the works.

In 1751, many of the tenants of Livingston were in rent arrears. Several of the tenants refused to pay on the grounds that their land belonged to the Commonwealth of Massachusetts, a ploy assisted by land speculators from the Commonwealth. On June 10, 1753, these Taconic tenants attempted to kidnap one of the foremen of the ironworks but were turned back by the Ancram tenants. Fear swept through the area as rumors spread that the Springfield, Massachusetts sheriff and 100 men would arrest all of the Ancram woodcutters and colliers. Livingston was worried that the loss of these woodsmen would prevent his furnace from reheating again since he had recently repaired it at a "considerable expense," and that upwards of "100 poor people I daily employ in and about the works, many of which at least 30 have families in the woods" would be in jeopardy. He further stated that he would consider "abandoning all [his] professions [there]" if the trouble with his tenants did not subside.

Two years later, on May 6, 1755, 103 rioters attacked Ancram and took 8 of the key men hostage. They destroyed the furnace where Livingston was engaged in "making Cannon shott & carriage wheels" for a military expedition against the French. He wrote to Governor Delancey in June as follows:

> My poor fellows whose familyes are in a starving condition [are] still in confinement, which has put it out of my power to furnish Messr Bankes & Dire hitherto with the Carrage wheels and Mr. William Alexander with the

The Albany Iron Works, which rolled the hull plates for the ironclad Monitor, *is shown here in 1861. The residential area that developed around the Burden Iron Works, Albany Iron Works, Troy Steel, and other iron companies was known as Scottsville.*

Quantity of shot, I engaged to deliver him for the Expedition to Onjagera [Niagara] & Crown Point, and yett nothwithstanding all this ill treatment I have received, as I had the Expedition very much at heart I ordered my furnace . . . to be immediately repaired at a great expense of upwards of £400 that I might still be able to furnish the Shott & c as soon as my workmen returned that the expeditions might not be retarded on that account, and I have now had her in good order since monday last, but no workmen yett, so that I cannot proceed in the Casting.

Livingston's men were finally returned in a prisoner exchange and cost him 50 pounds and more during the ordeal. That autumn, Livingston's carpenter was threatened by a group when he was repairing one of the ponds that supplied water to the ironworks during dry seasons, but this appears to have been the last problem at Ancram.

The lack of interest by Beekman and the troubles of Livingston served to damper any attempts to develop ironworks on the other manorial properties. Certainly the emotional frustration of Livingston must have been the topic of conversation among the other manor lords. If New York was going to develop a successful iron industry during the eighteenth century, it would not happen on manorial lands.

THE HUDSON VALLEY INDUSTRY

In 1737, while Governor Clark was urging the New York Assembly to promote iron, Cornelius Board was exploring the Ringwood-Sterling Pond region in the Ramapo Mountains of Orange County for precious metals like gold, silver, and copper. Board discovered outcroppings of iron ore at the southwest end of Sterling Lake. After purchasing 150 acres of the land from John Burnet, an East Jersey proprietor, Board and partner Timothy Ward erected a bloomery shortly after 1736. The ironworks was the first in a series that made the Ramapo area the leading iron-producing center in the state during the eighteenth century. The Hudson Highlands area had ample supplies of ore of nontitaniferous magnetites, which produced from 50 to 60 percent iron when smelted, abundant forests for charcoal production, sufficient waterpower, and a close New York City market.

Ironworks developed in the lower Hudson Valley during and after the American Revolution. In fact, many of the ironworks started by providing the Continental armies with supplies. Unfortunately, these ironmasters had little money, were not paid on time by the army, or had trouble supplying labor to the works and closed. Several important ironworks developed in the Ramapo region besides the Sterling works of Board and Ward. The Forest of Dean furnace began as early as 1756 and was 5 miles southeast of West Point. The Queensboro Furnace, near Fort Montgomery, was built prior to 1783. The Cedar Pond Forges, established by Samuel Brester, one of Rockland County's largest landholders, began sometime after 1767. An ironworks at Amenia in Dutchess County started in 1765. The Hasenclever ironworks at Cortland, Westchester County, began in 1766, and furnaces and bloomeries were erected on the manor of Phillipsburg in Westchester and Haverstraw in Rockland at the time of the Revolution.

The Sterling, Amenia, and Forest of Dean ironworks all supplied iron to the army, but not without difficulty. Sterling employed 180 men at the time of the Revolution and was producing more than 1,500 tons of pig iron. The increased production made necessary by army contracts created a labor shortage at the works. Sterling advertised that it needed 68 people just to run the furnace. The Forest of Dean furnace closed around 1799, but may have stopped producing iron in 1777, when the British captured nearby Fort Montgomery.

New York had no ironworks during the first half of the eighteenth century, yet, on the eve of the American Revolution, New York supplied one-third of the pig iron exported to England. New York went from exporting 1.5 percent in 1760 to 34 percent by 1775. In total, New York ironworks exported 11,250 tons of pig iron and 5,509 tons of bar iron to Great Britain between 1743 and 1776.

After the Revolution, several other ironworks developed in the Ramapo district, many of which lasted well into the nineteenth century. In 1800, Samuel Darter erected two forges on the Ramapo near Pleasantdale and employed 140 men, producing merchant iron for New York City. The Greenwood furnaces erected by James Cunigham in 1811 near Arden produced cannonballs for American forces during the War of 1812. Finally, the Southfield Furnaces, started in 1804 by the Townsend family, was an extension of the Sterling ironworks—then owned by the Townsend family. John and Isaiah Townsend were responsible for developing the first ironworks in Albany in 1807.

Around 1800, New York received a tremendous boost in the iron industry with the discovery of major deposits of hemetitic and limonitic iron ores in the Adirondack region of Upstate New York. Ironworks were soon erected, the first of which was built in 1801 to make anchors at Willsborough Falls on the Bocquet River in Essex County. The industry developed rapidly as furnaces were built at New Russia, Jay, and Elba in Essex County and the Eagle Rolling Mills in Keesville, Clinton County—all in the Champlain Valley district. Farther west, charcoal furnaces were built in Lawrence, Jefferson, Lewis, Otsego, and Oneida Counties.

Many of these ironworks, such as the Brasher, Waddington, Norfolk, and Westville furnaces in St. Lawrence County, used local bog iron ores (poor-grade hematite). By 1830, there were over 176 ironworks in the northern part of the state comprising blast furnaces, bloomeries, air furnaces, rolling mills, and naileries. These ironworks found a ready market in the Hudson-Mohawk region and farther south in New York City.

THE HUDSON-MOHAWK REGION

The Yankee invasion of the 1790s brought to the Hudson-Mohawk region several people familiar with iron making, as well as those who weren't familiar but were willing to learn. The Hudson-Mohawk region owes its iron history to people with names such as Corning, Norton, Townsend, Starbuck, and Winslow. The genius of these people and the position of the region as the terminus for the Champlain and Erie Canals were guarantees that the Albany-Troy area would become a major iron-producing center. These factors, combined with nature's large deposits of molding sand, limestone, and forests for charcoal in the region, were responsible for the Hudson Valley becoming one of eight places that produced all of the nation's iron by 1860.

In 1823, the completion of the Champlain Canal allowed access to the vast iron ore and pig iron of the north. Two years later, the Erie Canal opened between Albany and Buffalo, creating a western market. The arrival of large quantities of pig iron to the terminals of the canals for eventual shipment to New York City was an important factor in determining what types of ironworks developed in the Hudson-Mohawk region.

For example, it would be less expensive to buy Adirondack pig iron than import iron ore and produce charcoal and flux for local production. This might account for the fact that there were only two blast furnaces in the Albany-Troy area before the Civil War.

Instead, air or cupola furnaces, forges, and rail mills developed utilizing the available pig iron to manufacture stoves, machines, and railroad iron. The number of ironworks in the Capital District increased from 9 in 1810 to 20 in 1835, with a high of 41 ironworks in 1855. Rensselaer County had 18 in 1850 while Schenectady County had a high of 5. Albany County had a high of 27 ironworks in 1855.

A total of more than 226,000 tons of pig iron reached the Albany-Troy area between the years 1810 and 1860 from the canals. From 1844 to 1860, pig iron production from the Adirondacks was the primary supplier and some 190,949 tons were shipped down the

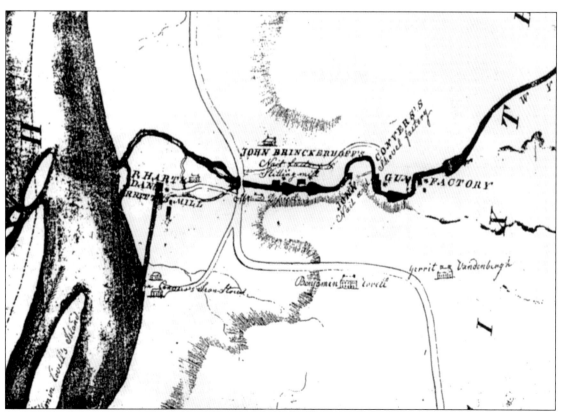

An early map shows John Brinkerhoff's nail factory on the Wyantskill in South Troy.

Champlain Canal to the Troy terminus. This figure is compared to 26,804 tons of pig iron shipped east to the Troy area on the Erie Canal for the same period. Much of this pig iron was used in the Albany-Troy industries while the remaining tonnage continued south to New York or other markets.

Coal was necessary for the fueling of the ironworks. Since there were no coal deposits in New York State, this important ingredient was imported early on from Ohio and Kentucky, and then from the mines of eastern Pennsylvania during the 1840s and 1850s. Anthracite was shipped to Albany and Troy by way of the Erie Canal and Delaware and Hudson Canal. During the 1840s and 1850s, railroads began shipping coal to market as well. Anthracite came to Albany-Troy from the Mauch Chunk mines of the Schuylkill Basin and from the Scranton and Pittston mines of the Wyoming and Lackawanna Basin, Pennsylvania. Bituminous coal came to Albany-Troy from the Bloosburg Barclay, Piedmont-Cumberland, and Broad Top mines of Pennsylvania.

Troy's Iron Age

Troy excelled in the production of cast-iron stoves, pig, ironware, iron and steel products, wire, nails, spikes, horseshoes, bloom and bar, and railroad iron.

Troy's first ironworks was a nail factory on the banks of the Wyantskill. Built in 1807 by John Brinkerhoff of Albany, it had 11 cutting and heading machines by 1824. Erastus Corning of Albany purchased the nail factory in 1826 and renamed it the Albany Nail Factory. Corning, who later became an iron magnate and president of the New York Central Railroad, began his career in a Troy hardware store. In 1830, the factory rolled 825 tons of iron, of which 450 tons were cut into nails and the rest for other products. By 1839, the company became the Albany Iron Works and wrought iron was first made there. A steam works was added as well as a water mill; forge; machine and blacksmith shop; spike, bolts and rivet factory; and even a mechanics hall.

It was at the Albany Iron Works that the iron plates were rolled for the USS *Monitor*, the ironclad that faced the Confederate ironclad CSS *Virginia/Merrimack* in a well-known Civil War battle at Hampton Roads in Virginia on March 9, 1862.

Not far from the Albany Iron Works was the Bessemer Steel Works. Alexander Holly, John A. Griswold, and John F. Winslow purchased the rights to this English invention to convert pig iron to steel, and the first Bessemer steel in the country was made on February 16, 1865.

Others iron mills were erected along the Wyantskill, including the Rensselaer Iron Works, a rolling mill, but it was the Burden Iron Company that gave Troy world fame.

In 1809, John Converse and his partners erected a rolling and slitting mill on the upper falls of the Wyantskill. It became the Troy Iron and Nail Factory a few years later and had, besides the nail factory and mill, other shops and about 50 houses, which one writer named Adamsville after Colonel Nathaniel Adams. In 1822, Henry Burden became superintendent. In 1825, he received a patent for a wrought nail and spike machine that increased production. A few years later, in 1834, he patented a machine to make countersunk railroad spikes. The following year, his patented horseshoe-making machine made 15 to 20 horseshoes a minute, and this would become Burden's legacy. He continually refined his inventions until he had a machine that could make a horseshoe in one motion. By 1848, Burden owned the company, and in 1881, he renamed it the Burden Iron Company.

During the Civil War, Burden's horseshoes were on the hooves of most of the Northern army's horses. The Confederates also wanted them and ordered their troops to try and grab any shipments. The Southern forces also employed a spy from Canada to go to Troy and obtain the specifications of the machines so that they could be made in Atlanta. Neither plan worked. The company produced 51 million horseshoes annually in its heyday.

Of particular interest, Burden Iron Works operated the largest waterwheel in the country, at 60 feet in diameter, 22 feet wide, and with 36 buckets. Many believe that RPI graduate George Ferris modeled the design of his 36-seat Ferris wheel amusement ride on Burden's waterwheel.

Henry Burden's inventive character made him one of the biggest iron producers in the country. Burden's iron works produced 51 million horseshoes a year.

Workers pose in Fuller & Warren's grinding room.

Ironworks also sprang up along the Poestenkill north of the Wyantskill. While the Wyantskill provided waterpower for huge rolling mills and works like Burden, Bessemer, and Albany Iron Works, the Poestenkill provided power for smaller operations like wire, machine, and file works, in addition to flour, cotton, planing, and paper mills. These mills were powered by an elaborate hydraulic power system created by Benjamin Marshall that included a tunnel drilled through 600 feet of solid rock.

KEEPING THE WORLD WARM

During the period between 1790 and 1850, Troy grew in size from a mere few hundred residents to almost 30,000 people.

More than 400 patents were issued to Capital District inventors. Albany, Troy's chief rival, led the pack with 157 patents, but Troy was not far behind at 132. However, between 1809 and 1850, 123 out of 479 patents issued in the Capital District had to do with cast-iron stoves or furnaces. Thirty-one patents out of 132 in Troy were issued to 23 different Trojans for inventions relating to this industry. In Albany, 53 stove-related patents were issued to 33 Albanians. Keeping people warm was certainly on the minds of many inventors.

In 1815, William T. James of Lansingburgh patented the first cookstove, called the "Baltimore Cookstove." It was made and sold in Troy. Most stoves up to that time were imported as plates from Pennsylvania and New Jersey, then assembled and sold in Troy as finished product.

That all changed with the establishment of the Troy Air Furnace in 1818, on the southeast corner of Fifth and Grand Division Streets, and the Eagle Furnace in 1823, at 42 Fifth Avenue, as well as other iron foundries that processed their own iron, either from scratch or from imported pig iron. The Starbuck brothers, Charles and Nathaniel, began casting stoves in Troy as early as 1821 with partner Ephraim Gurley.

Troy soon became a leader in cast-iron stove production. In 1829, two foundries produced $120,000 worth of stoves. By 1855, there were 7 foundries, employing a total of 670 men and producing 75,000 stoves. By 1875, 23 stove companies were producing more than $4 million worth of stoves and employing more than 2,000 men. By 1888, only five were left, but they were producing $2 million worth of stoves.

Troy stoves can still be found (and are still being used) around the world with associated names such as Fuller & Warren; Bussey & McLeod; Burdett, Smith, & Co.; George W.

This Fuller & Warren cast-iron stove is of the "Onward no. 4" style.

Swett; Quimby & Perry, Geer; Cox, Eddy; Ingals; Torrance; Burtis; and many more. One historian wrote that llamas carried Troy stoves across the "Andes to the western coast of South America," and that even camels carried them to "the shores of the Black Sea in Asia, and ships to Ireland and North Europe, Turkey, China, Japan, Australia, and in fact, to nearly all parts of the civilized world."

One of the more famous stove makers was Fuller & Warren from South Troy. This stove maker, known as the Clinton Stove Works, comprised 6 acres of land on the Hudson below River Street between Madison and Monroe Streets. In the 1876 World Centennial Exhibition, in Philadelphia, one of their stoves won a special award for beauty. Several of the foundry buildings still exist, and they are the only remaining physical testament that this worldwide supplier of stoves ever existed in Troy.

It was at Fuller & Warren that Philo Penfield Stewart, inventor of the ultimate cooking stove, gained his fame. In fact, Fuller & Warren stoves, no matter what they looked like, were known as "Stewart" stoves. Fuller & Warren bought the Stewart patents in 1859.

The second-largest stove maker in Troy was the Empire Stove Works, erected in 1846 and located on Second and Ida Streets along the Poestenkill. Empire was started by Anson Atwood in 1841. Anson was an early stove inventor with four patents from 1838 to 1845, which included a summer cooking stove (1838), a railway cooking stove (1839), a new design for a cooking stove (1842), and an airtight stove (1845). George W. Swett took over this works, and by 1886, the company was producing stoves with a worldwide reputation.

Many of the stoves were replaced by furnaces in the later half of the nineteenth and early twentieth centuries. But for nearly a century, millions of people around the world were warmed by Troy stoves that had been invented or improved by the following Trojans: Anson Atwood, C.H. Rogers and S.H. Hancox, Caleb Slade, Daniel Williams, D.B. Cox, Eben Eaton, Eli C. Robinson, Elias Johnson, Elihu Smith, Ezra Ripley, J.B. Challar, E. Jones, James Wager, John Morrison, John T. Davey, Peter Low, Rensselaer D. Granger, Samuel Hanley, Samuel Pierce, and Sylvester Parker. Ezra Ripley patented the first teakettle in Troy in 1846.

TROY'S RINGING HISTORY

For thousands of years, bells have served in various capacities in most civilized cultures. They have been used to signal time, human passings, and natural disasters. Bells have been used to communicate and have been played as musical instruments. They have been part of the rituals of religious institutions for centuries. Even today, many ancient Chinese bells, some more than 3,000 years old, have been functional from the time of the Shang and Zhou dynasties.

While bells have been part of humanity's tool box, some of the finest sounding bells were cast in Troy and across the river at West Troy (Watervliet) during the nineteenth and twentieth centuries. Thousands of Troy bells, known for their quality of sound and workmanship, still grace church towers and other institutions around the world. Yet, this local industry that served the world consisted of no more than four companies and was pretty much a family affair: the Meneely family (which owned two different companies), Julius Hanks, and Jones and Company.

The Jones Bell Foundry was located on the southeast corner of First and Adams. The firm dissolved in May 1887.

Troy's first bell caster, Julius Hanks, was the son of Benjamin Hanks, who built the first bell foundry in America. Julius moved his manufactory of scientific instruments from Watervliet (then Gibbonsville) to the corner of Fifth and Fulton in Troy in 1825. Besides church bells, Hanks began to make town clocks and surveyor's instruments. In 1833, he received a patent for a compass and magnetic needle.

One of Hanks employees, William Gurley was a graduate from Rensselaer Institute. He later established, on the same site, a manufacturing company of surveyor's instruments, which became famous for their engineering and quality. The Gurley Building still stands at this location.

When Hanks operated his foundry in Gibbonsville, Andrew Meneely, the son of Irish immigrants, became an apprentice there, learned the trade, and later purchased the foundry after Hanks moved to Troy. Andrew also married the niece of Julius Hanks's cousin Horatio. Andrew's sons, George and Edwin, took over the business in 1851 when Andrew died.

The Meneely brothers gained a reputation for excellent quality, and George Meneely was awarded a patent for a method of attaching bells to a yoke that permitted the bell to turn; this allowed the clapper to hit all parts of the bell instead of one spot, thereby avoiding the chance of cracking, a fate that befell the Liberty Bell. In fact, it was the Meneely foundry that cast the replacement for the Liberty Bell during the country's centennial celebration in 1876. It is this bell that now hangs in Independence Hall in Philadelphia; the original, cracked bell lies opposite the hall in a special exhibit.

The famous Burden iron wheel, built in 1838–1839, was 60 feet in diameter, 22 feet wide, had 36 buckets that were each 6 foot, 3 inches deep, and provided an output of 1200 horsepower. Called the "Niagara of Water-wheels," it is thought to have been the inspiration for the invention of the Ferris wheel by bridge builder George Ferris, an RPI graduate. The first Ferris wheel appeared at the 1893 World's Colombian Exposition in Chicago. It, too, had 36 "buckets," or seats.

A brother-in-law of Andrew Meneely, James Harvey Hitchcock, left the employ of the company, and along with Eber Jones, created a competing bell company, Jones and Hitchcock, later Jones and Company, in 1852. While they gave Meneely a run for their money, they went out of business only 35 years later. One of their last castings was the tower bell that was placed in the old city hall on the corner of Third and State.

A third son of Andrew Meneely, Clinton Hanks Meneely, entered the bell-making business in Troy with George H. Kimberley on River and Adams Streets directly across the river from his brothers. This created a feud that lasted for years, including a court case to force Clinton not to use the Meneely name. The West Troy Meneelys lost the case.

Both Meneely companies produced thousands of bells, over 350 chimes (8 or more bells), and a few carillons (23 or more bells) until they both went out of business in the early 1950s. Their bells still ring, however.

According to Joe Connors, a chime historian who not only can play them but has videotaped many, said that the surviving chimes located in Troy churches were made by both Meneely foundries. Holy Cross Episcopal (only six bells), Woodside Presbyterian (key of G), Ascension Episcopal (key of G), and St. John's Episcopal (probably F or G, originally) have sets cast by the Meneelys of West Troy. St. John's Episcopal (E flat), St.

Peter's (E flat), St Joseph's (E flat), and St. Patrick's Roman Catholic (E flat) churches all have chimes cast by Clinton Meneely of Troy.

P. Thomas Carroll, executive director of the Hudson Mohawk Industrial Gateway, reported that close to 100,000 bells were produced in this area, and most are probably still out there. And according to Connors, almost 70 percent of the chimes made in the country were made by the two Meneely and the Jones bell companies, making this area the premier bell-casting region in the country.

Interestingly, the Meneely foundries had other differences—the actual tone of their bells. According to musicologist Dis Maley Jr., who has perfect pitch and has listened to many of the local bells, Andrew Meneely's bells seemed to have been tuned to the keys of F or G, while Clinton Meneely's bells were in the key of E flat. Maley also stated that the Clinton bells were heavier, sounding stronger, but have undertones in the higher bells. Clinton apparently cast his bells exactly to specifications, but did not tune them afterward. Andrew's bells, which were lighter after 1922, were tuned after casting if they were off key. According to Maley, this gave Andrew's bells a bit more musical quality than Clinton's products. Whether this tonal difference was done on purpose—Clinton trying to differentiate his work from his brothers—is unknown and worthy of further study.

All physical evidence of bell making in Troy, except for the Jones Bell Foundry, are gone, and this last remaining foundry building is slated for demolition in the near future.

Ludlow workers pour a 60-inch valve in 1906.

10. Troy Becomes the Collar City

One may remember the television commercial of old that shows a woman complaining about "ring around the collar" and using a detergent to wash out the grime from her husband's shirt. "Ring around the collar" isn't simply a Madison Avenue executive's clever ploy to sell washing detergent. It is a centuries-old problem, and more than 150 years ago, a Troy woman set out to do something about it. However, she hadn't planned on creating a whole new industry.

Hannah Lord was the daughter of William A. Lord, a Revolutionary War officer, assembly member, and the author of *Lord's Military Tactics*. She married Orlando Montague, a shoemaker (or blacksmith), on August 14, 1817, and both settled in Troy, originally on Second Street.

Mrs. Montague, tired of washing her husband's shirts because only the collars were dirty, decided one day to snip off a collar, wash it, and sew it back on. Mr. Montague, it is written, agreed to the experiment, and in 1827, the first detachable collar was made at their home at 139 Third Street (recently torn down).

Notice of the event spread throughout the city. The Reverend Ebenezer Brown, formerly a Methodist minister, was then the owner of a small notions shop at 285 River Street, and he was asked several times for the new product, about which news was buzzing around the streets of the city.

Brown saw the need and rushed to fill it. His wife and daughter began cutting, stitching, and laundering the first detachable collars, consisting of two-ply material, which had to be taped and tied around the neck. These early collars were called "string collars" and cost 25¢ a piece, or $2 per dozen. Brown sold and delivered the collars door to door.

His popularity forced him to set up a workshop in the back of his store, where he hired several women to do the job, and also outsourced the work. Payment for the women's labor was in the form of "trade" in his store and was set by his own price. This may have been the first "sweat shop." Brown eventually moved to New York City in 1834.

Orlando Montague, the first person to wear a detachable collar, soon began his own competitive collar factory with business partner Austin Granger in 1834. The Montague & Granger collar factory began production at 222 River Street. Besides improving on the string collar, they developed the "Bishop" collar, an upright modification of the turn-down collar. Besides collars, they manufactured "dickeys" (detached shirt bosoms) and separate cuffs.

96

Hannah Lord Montague created the first detachable collar.

Detachable collars had the problem of leaving gaps between the shirt and collar, and this led to the invention of the use of buttons to snap the collars in place. This improvement also led to the development of several new collar designs.

Mrs. Montague's original reason for creating the first detachable collar was to clean it separately from the shirt. With the increased production of collars came the need to wash the thousands of collars being produced. In 1835, Independence Starks entered the collar-making business and also created the first Troy Laundry at 66 North Second Street (Fifth Avenue), where he washed not only his own collars, but those of competitors as well. Many years later, the laundry industry sparked the creation of the first female union in the country.

The year 1835 was also the same year that carpenter Lyman Bennett entered the collar industry. He created the "collar express," an assembly line production for making collars. His wife cut the cloth into shapes, and he carried them to various homes of other women who would stitch, starch, turn, button hole, and iron them. The cut collars were tied in bundles and delivered via wagons, the "collar express." Boys were hired at $1.50 a week to deliver the collars throughout Troy and environs. Bennett, called the "Father of the Collar Industry" by one historian, moved his business to 344 River in 1853 along with new partners M.W. Hicks & O.W. Edson, becoming Bennett, Hicks & Edson, linen manufacturers.

The year 1845 marked the beginning of the major production of detachable cuffs and shirt making in the city. While shirts were not invented in Troy, the first shirt maker was

Lawrence Van Valkenburgh, who was located on the southeast corner of Seventh Avenue and Fulton Street.

With the introduction of machines used for sewing, button holing, folding, and turning, the basis for centralized production factories was established, although many collars were still made by hand from private homes. In 1852, Jefferson Gardner was the first to try sewing machines made by Wheeler & Wilson & Co. to stitch collars at his Gardner & White shop at 335 River Street.

Women who had been making 50¢ a day stitching collars and cuffs by hand were now making $2.50 a day thanks to the sewing machine. In 1855, the firm of Bennett & Edson powered these sewing machines with steam. For the next 50 years, many inventions were developed to aid the collar, cuff, and shirt industry, and Troy production boomed. By the late 1880s, detachable collars were being manufactured around the nation.

By the early twentieth century, 15,000 people worked in the collar industry in Troy, and more than 85 percent were native-born women. Ninety out of every 100 collars worn in America were made in the city, and Troy became world famous as the "Collar City."

In 1901, there were 26 collar and cuff makers and 38 laundries in the city. Wearing a detached white collar gave rise to a new working social class, the "white collar" workers who differentiated themselves from the no or "blue" collar factory workers. However, by 1962, only six companies were still making collars and cuffs in Troy, and by the 1970s, most had gone out of business or moved south.

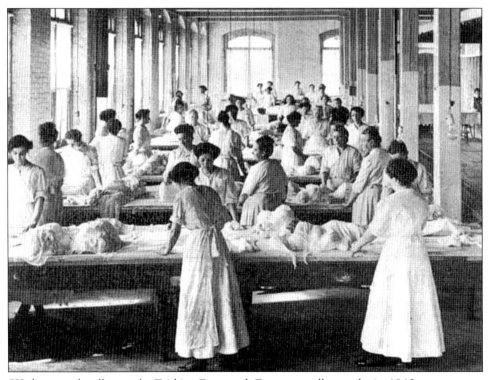

Workers starch collars at the Frisbie, Coon and Company collar works in 1912.

The firm Maullin & Bigelow partnered with George B. Cluett in 1861. Several years and many partnerships later, in 1901, the firm became Cluett, Peabody and Company and is still in business, although they moved out of Troy in 1990. Cluett, Peabody and Co. became the nation's leading collar maker in 1907, a position they held for 24 years due to a successful advertising campaign featuring the "Arrow Man," illustrated by J.C. Leyendecker (see Chapter 13). It was not until 1935 that the company abandoned collars, finally reacting to the fact that shirts with attached collars had become standard.

As a student at RPI, Sanford L. Cluett (1874–1968) invented a bubble sextant for celestial navigation. In 1919, he joined Cluett, Peabody and Co., which was founded by his uncles. During the late 1920s, detachable shirt collars were going out of fashion and the shirts the company was making with permanently attached collars looked terrible after being washed. Cluett felt that the pulling action during shirt manufacturing had to be balanced with a pushing counteraction, and he designed a machine on which cloth was passed over a contracting elastic felt blanket. The process was named for him, becoming known as Sanforizing.

Cluett also invented Clupak, a stretchable paper that was difficult to tear. The process he developed enhances the burst, stretch, and cross-machine tear properties of paper while retaining its tensile strength. This invention has found extensive use in shopping bags and in wrapping paper (Kraft paper) for magazines, catalogs, tires, meat, and furniture. At the time of his death, Cluett had been awarded more than 200 patents, and his Sanforized cloth was licensed by 448 mills in 58 countries.

The last existing firm that has collar roots, Marvin Neitzel Corporation, goes back to 1886, when E.W. Marvin joined the firm Gunnison & Son, which made ladies linen collars and cuffs at 11 Fourth Street. Marvin changed the name Gunnison & Marvin and later incorporated the business in 1908 as E.W. Marvin Company. Raymond P. Neitzel joined the firm in 1917, helping to develop a full line of hospital products, and the firm became Marvin Neitzel Corporation in 1931. The corporation was the last to make collars in Troy, ceasing collar production only a few years ago. The company continued making nurses uniforms but finally went out of business in 2002.

A few of Troy's most notable collar companies are as follows: Ball Brothers; C.H. McClellan; Cooperative Collar & Cuff Company; Corliss, Coon & Co.; C.W. Ferguson Collar Company; Earl & Wilson; Fellows & Co.; Gardner & White; George P. Ide & Company; Hall, Hartwell & Company; H.C. Curtis & Co.; Joseph Bowman & Sons; J. Stettheimer Jr. & Co.; Tim & Co.; United Shirt & Collar Company; Wilbur, Miller & Wilbur; Wood & Lewis, to name just a few. Many of these firms changed names and owners, merged with others, or moved to other places over the years.

In today's telephone books, there no longer is a heading for the collar industry. Fortunately, several of the large manufacturing buildings remain standing as a testament to this important local industry.

DON'T IRON WHILE THE STRIKE IS HOT

During the nineteenth century, working 15 hours a day was the norm in industrial cities like Troy and Cohoes. Not only did entire families work in factories, in many cases,

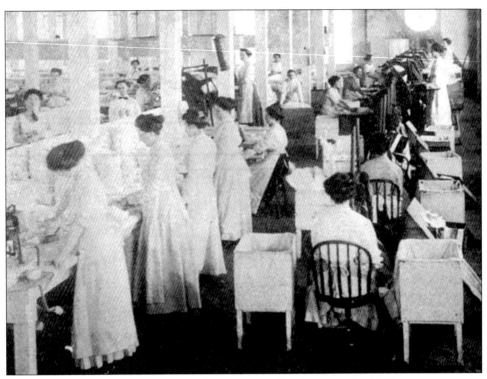

These women iron collars by hand at the Troy Laundry Company in 1912.

safety conditions were deplorable. In 1884, the Federation of Organized Trades and Labor Unions passed a resolution stating that eight hours constituted a legal day's work from and after May 1, 1886. They called a national strike on that day, and more than 350,000 workers across the country responded. May Day became an annual celebration.

But what led up to that event? In Troy, where the collar and cuff industry was preeminent, mostly women worked in the industry making collars, cuffs, shirts, and cleaning them. None of these jobs were particularly risk free. The collar maids worked with hard chemicals and acids, machines that could peel skin off in seconds, and belt-driven machinery that could decapitate one sitting at the device.

One of the most taxing jobs of the nineteenth century was the collar laundry. Soap was handmade from caustic lyes and fat. The fire that made soap was created by chopping wood and hauling vats of water. Starch had to be made—not sprayed from a can—and spot removal meant real elbow grease. In Troy, there were some 15 different laundries.

Nineteen-year-old Kate Mullaney was one of the 3,000 women in Troy who worked in the collar industry during the 1860s. Kate, her mother, sister Mary, two younger sisters, and brother Frank, all Irish immigrants, lived not far from the collar center around River Street. In 1864, Kate, along with coworkers Esther Keegan and Sarah McQuillan, decided that the laundry workers deserved more money and better working conditions. They formed the Collarworkers Union, the first female union in the country with staying power, with the encouragement of the powerful Troy Iron Molders' Union No. 2.

At noon, on Wednesday, February 23, 1864, 300 or so women went on strike from all the commercial laundries. The owners gave in almost a week later. Kate Mullaney and her union led a few more successful strikes, and even created a cooperative, the Union Line Collar and Cuff Manufactory, before finally being beaten by the owners in 1870. However, Kate opened many doors for working women.

In 1867 and 1869, the Cigar and Printers Unions allowed women as members. In 1869, Augusta Lewis, another woman labor leader and president of the Women's Typographical Union, said of the Troy Collar Laundry Union, "Others will be encouraged by their success and will be stimulated by their examples to elevate their own condition."

That same year, a group of women shoe stitchers in Lynn, Massachusetts, organized the Daughters of St. Crispin, a national women's labor organization modeled on (and supported by) the Knights of St. Crispin, a national shoe workers union. The Daughters of St. Crispin is recognized as the first national union of women. Also, Alzina Parsons Stevens, a typographer, organized the Working Woman's Union No. 1 in 1877. In 1890, Josephine Shaw Lowell organized the Consumers' League of New York.

William Sylvis, president of the national union, appointed Kate Mullaney the assistant secretary in 1868, making her the first woman ever appointed to a national union office. From 1869 to 1875, Kate and her family lived in a three-story, brick double-row house on Eighth Street near Hoosick. She died on Friday, August 17, 1906, and was buried in an unmarked grave at St. Peter's Cemetery. Recently, union members and interested people raised money to erect a Celtic cross on her unmarked grave during a Labor Day celebration. On July 15, 1998, First Lady Hillary Clinton placed a plaque on the house honoring her efforts.

Marvin Neitzel, then on Federal and Fifth Avenues, was the last collar maker in Troy.

11. TROY IN THE CIVIL WAR

Trojans have participated in every war from the Revolutionary War to more modern conflicts. They have provided men and women for combat, for the production of war materials, and have even invented items that turned out to help win wars.

The citizens of Troy played an important role during the time leading up to and during America's Civil War. Trojans were in leadership positions in the military as well as on the firing line. Many gave their lives, and Trojans at home abolished slavery early and took part in the Underground Railroad, a network to smuggle slaves from the South to freedom. Moreover, several Troy industries did their part in the manufacture of war materials, including building the hull plates for the ironclad USS *Monitor*, which participated in what many historians claim was the turning point for the North during the war.

Slavery was introduced in New York in 1626, when 11 people were brought in as forced labor. When the federal government conducted its first census in 1790, there were 1,474 slave-holding families in Albany County (Rensselaer County was part of Albany County until 1791) who owned 3,722 slaves. At least 23 of those families had 10 to19 slaves each. By 1800, Rensselaer County listed 890 slaves, decreasing to 750 in 1810, down to 433 by 1820, and by 1830, there were none. Slavery was abolished in the state in 1827. On the reverse side, there were 632 free slaves living here in 1820, increasing to 1,058 free slaves before the Civil War began. So, for 30 years before the Civil War, there were no slaves living in the Capital District.

Many people, especially in the Northern states, believed it was wrong to own another human being. The abolitionist movement during the three decades prior to the Civil War made the slavery question the prime concern of national politics and quickened the demise of slavery in America. But the end of slavery began much earlier.

In 1774, Connecticut and Rhode Island banned the importation of slaves. In 1776, the Society of Friends (Quakers) abolished slavery among its members. The following year, Vermont prohibited slavery. By 1780, Massachusetts adopted a freedom clause interpreted as prohibiting slavery. Pennsylvania adopted gradual emancipation. In 1784, Connecticut and Rhode Island also passed gradual emancipation laws. Four years later, Connecticut prohibited residents from participating in the slave trade.

On March 29, 1799, New York State passed a gradual emancipation law declaring that after July 4, 1799, every child born to a slave within the state would be free, although he/she would remain with the owner, mother, executors, or assigns until the age of 28

This is the 1795 document that freed Elkanah Watson's slave Sarah March. There were no slaves in Rensselaer County by 1830.

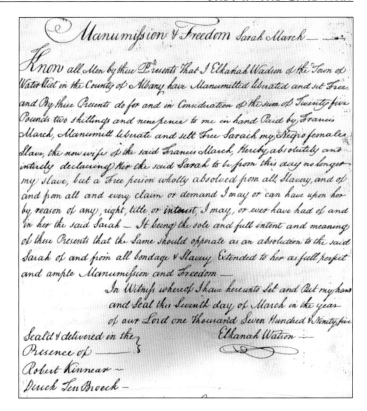

if male, or 25, if female. Every black person born before July 4, 1799, was free after July 4, 1827.

In the Capital District, slaves were set free, or manumitted, as early as 1795. Elkanah Watson freed one of his slaves, Sarah March, and recorded the deed in the minutes of the Town of Watervliet. Many other manumissions are recorded from other slaveholders, as well.

Troy played its role as part of the Underground Railroad, a loosely formed network of sympathetic whites, free slaves, and anyone else wanting to help smuggle Southern slaves to Canada or other Northern states. The Underground Railroad actually began during the late colonial period as a reaction to the Fugitive Slave Act of 1793, which provided for the return of escaped black slaves between states.

The law was hardly enforced in the North since slavery was being abolished, but as a concession to the South, a second and stronger fugitive slave law was passed as part of the Compromise of 1850. This law was tested in Troy ten years later.

In November 1834, the new Liberty Street Presbyterian Church was being dedicated on the north side of Liberty Street between Third and Fourth Streets. Its new pastor, the Reverend Henry Highland Garnet, was brought in from Oberlin College and stayed for several years. Garnet was born a slave in New Market, Maryland, in 1815 and escaped in 1824, making his way to New York, where he studied at the Oneida Theological Institute in Whitesboro, before becoming a Presbyterian minister.

103

After his arrest in 1860, escaped slave Charles Nalle was taken to the building of the Mutual National Bank of Troy on First and State Streets. The U.S. commissioners office was on the second floor.

While Garnet was in Troy, he formulated strong anti-slavery views. Garnet delivered a "Call to Rebellion" at the National Negro Convention in Buffalo, New York, in 1843, encouraging African Americans to resist slavery by means of armed rebellion. At the party convention for the Liberty Party in Buffalo, Garnet served on the nominating committee—the first time African Americans participated directly in the conventions.

The abolitionist movement took off in the 1830s, partly as a result of the evangelical movement that swept the North beginning in the 1820s. It not only called for the end of slavery but also for women's rights. By 1838, more than 1,350 anti-slavery societies existed, with almost 250,000 members, including many women.

An adaptation of Harriet Beecher Stowe's book *Uncle Tom's Cabin*, which became an effective piece of abolitionist propaganda, was first performed in America in Troy in 1852 in Peale's Museum, on the corner of Fulton and River Street.

The fugitive slave acts were detested. When a runaway slave was captured, he or she was taken before a federal court or commissioner, denied a jury trial, and his/her testimony was not admitted. Only the statement of the master claiming ownership, even if absent, was taken as the main evidence. Obviously unfair, new personal-liberty laws contradicting the legislation of 1850 were passed in most of the Northern states. Abolitionists openly defied the 1850 act.

Northern newspapers reported several episodes where citizens took it upon themselves to help runaway slaves. More than 1,000 soldiers had to be used to guard escaped Virginia slave Anthony Burns in Boston when Bostonians failed to free him after they stormed the federal courthouse. A riot broke out in Lancaster County, Pennsylvania, when a federal official ordered Quaker bystanders to help catch a runaway—they didn't. The Quakers were prosecuted, but not convicted.

In Troy, there is the famous case of Charles Nalle. Nalle was a coachman for Uri Gilbert, a Troy businessman and later mayor. At the age of 28, Nalle escaped from plantation master Blucher W. Hasbrough of Culpepper County, Virginia, on October 19, 1848. Nalle made it to Rensselaer County and first worked for William Scram at Sand Lake as a teamster. He told his secret to Horace F. Averill, a lawyer in Sand Lake who notified Hasbrough. Nalle was arrested on April 27, 1860, and was brought to the U.S. commissioner's office on the second floor of the building at the corner of First and State. Several hundred people, including the legendary Harriet Tubman, waited for Nalle to be brought out. They rescued him from the commissioner's office and took him to the woods in Niskayuna, and later Amsterdam, before they eventually bought his freedom for $650. He returned to Troy a free man.

The Underground Railroad, a network of people opposed to slavery prior to the Civil War, was quite active in the Capital District. The area was a major location for helping funnel runaway slaves north to their freedom. While many in the Underground Railroad did their work behind the scenes, research from groups like Albany's Underground Railroad Workshop and others are revealing that many of the participants were quite "public" about their work.

Several people, from all walks of life, locally participated in the Underground Railroad movement as individuals or members of anti-slavery groups called "vigilance committees." Albanians included Reverend John Sands of the Second Wesleyan Church (African); Edward Delavan, owner, Delavan House; William Topp, black tailor; Dr. Thomas Elkins, black pharmacist; Minos McGowan, lumber merchant; Lydia and Abigail Mott, Quaker sisters; Captain Abraham Johnson, black ferryboat operator; barber William Henry Johnson; Stephen Myers; and many others.

Stephen Myers published the *Northern Star and Freeman's Advocate*, an arm of the Northern Star Association, a vigilance committee, and it appears he became the local leader of Underground Railroad operations. The Reverend Able Brown from Sand Lake published the *Tocsin of Liberty (Albany Patriot)* and listed the slaves he helped to free (over 1,000). Reverend Charles T. Torrey, who assisted Reverend Brown, was a white abolitionist, and he became a martyr for the abolition cause after a trial in 1844; he died in jail in 1846.

The following, taken from a letter carried by a runaway from Reverend Brown (which he signed as "cor Secy of Eastern N.Y. Aslavery Socy") to his Vermont friend Charles Hicks, an Underground Railroad operator near Bennington, says it all: "Dear Sir, Please receive the Bearer as a friend who needs your aid and direct him on his way if you cannot give him work he come to us well recommended was a slave a few weeks since."

Albany's General William L. Chaplin was also an agent of the New York Anti-Slavery Society. Chaplin took over Torrey's job as local correspondent of the *Albany Patriot* and an Underground Railroad conductor. In 1850, members of the U.S. Congress from Georgia arrested Torrey in Rockville, Maryland, with two other men who had been held in slavery.

Chaplin was held on bail, and married Theodosia Gilbert, business partner of James Caleb Jackson, while incarcerated. He escaped north after friends posted bail. Gilbert's partner, Jackson, was the editor of the *Albany Patriot* and the *Liberty Press*, both abolitionist papers.

Another Underground Railroad engineer was a Jesuit priest named John J. Kelley, who served both Albany and Troy. He is credited with writing the following broadside around 1850:

> We call on our fellow citizens, here and elsewhere, to aid us in funds to help the poor, unfortunate fugitives who come to us daily, in many cases destitute of clothing, weary of traveling and hungry. We appeal to the sympathy of ladies and gentlemen everywhere. We are in want of material aid and cast off clothing. All funds forwarded to Stephen Myers, William H. Topp, or any gentleman of the committee will be faithfully applied. All letters directed to this office will be duly answered.

This broadside also stated that 287 fugitives were helped through Albany in the ten months prior to July 15, 1856. It also listed the members of the committee as well as an address for the group—198 Lumber Street (Livingston Avenue).

George L. Aiken penned the dramatic version of Uncle Tom's Cabin *and played the characters of George Harris and George Shelby in the first Troy production.*

The vigilance committee kept watch for "slave catchers," or "man hunters," coming into the area looking for runaways. Members would let fugitives know that the hunters were in the area. Many fugitives who were working on farms or in businesses would then go into hiding.

There is less known about Underground Railroad activities in Rensselaer County. In addition to Father Kelley, there was the Reverend Fayette Shipherd. Reverend Shipherd (1797–1878) and his brother John Jay Shipherd (1802–1844) were Congregational ministers and active abolitionists. Reverend Shipherd, in a letter to the same Charles Hicks in Vermont, suggested strongly that the Champlain Canal should be a northern route to Canada from Troy. In 1842, he wrote, "As the canal has closed I shall send my Southern friends along your road & patronize your house." He further states, "We had 22 [slaves] in two weeks 13 in the city at one time."

Henry Highland Garnet, a Troy resident in the 1840s, gained a national and international reputation as an anti-slavery reformer at the Liberty Street Presbyterian Church. Also in the Troy area was John H. Hooper, a black fugitive from Maryland. His Troy home served as an Underground Railroad station. The Fox mansion in Sand Lake was also a haven for runaways. Troy native R. Johnson of Sand Lake, a Mr. Willigman, James G. Stewart, William Rich (listed as a hair dresser in the city directory on Fulton), and Charles Morton were also noted supporters of the Underground Railroad. Researchers have identified more than 60 local sites with Underground Railroad connections.

The book *Uncle Tom's Cabin* has been often labeled as the kindling wood of the Civil War. Written in 1852 by Harriet Beecher Stowe, a child of a Protestant preacher, it was originally penned as a set of articles for the Washington anti-slavery weekly, the *National Era*.

A teacher and the mother of seven children, Stowe wrote to support her family. This included poetry, travel guides, biographies, children's books, and adult novels. Yet, her name is forever etched in the annals of history with those who spoke out against slavery during the pre–Civil War period.

Uncle Tom's Cabin piqued public interest on the subject of slavery, but it was also based on Stowe's own life experiences growing up next to the slave state of Kentucky. Stowe had firsthand knowledge about the practice of slavery, the anti-slavery movement, and the Underground Railroad.

The book aroused intense controversy and made Stowe a national celebrity. To help dispel the attacks on her work, she published *A Key to Uncle Tom's Cabin* the following year, documenting the book's truths. She followed up with another anti-slavery novel, *Dred*, in 1856. Upon meeting Stowe in 1862, President Abraham Lincoln is reported to have greeted her as "the little woman who wrote the book that started this great war."

The first public performance of *Uncle Tom's Cabin* in America occurred in Troy on September 27, 1852, on the stage of Peale's Museum, on the corner of Fulton and River. It was a family production, performed mostly by the relatives of actor George C. Howard, the museum manager. His wife, Caroline, four-year-old daughter Cordelia, and George himself played the major characters. George Aiken, Howard's cousin, penned the dramatic version. Another actor in the play was William J. Le Moyne, who later went on to become a national stage star specializing in the works of Charles Dickens.

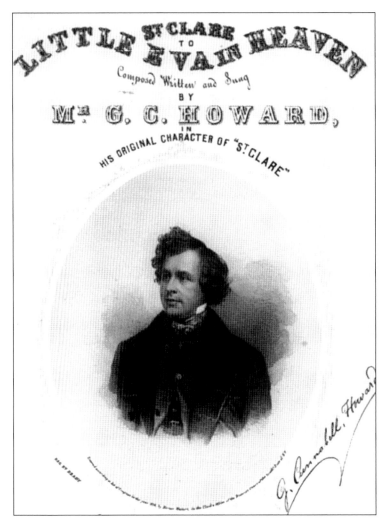

George C. Howard wrote all the music and played the character of St. Clare for the first production of Uncle Tom's Cabin.

The script ran 3 hours and 15 minutes, but only took the story up through little Eva's death. In November, Aiken rewrote the play and ended it with Stowe's finale. The two scripts were combined that month into a drama of six acts, which became the standard acting version of the play. It was so popular in Troy that it ran for 150 consecutive nights.

The play was performed continuously in the United States for 80 years. The Howards appeared in *Uncle Tom's Cabin* until 1857, when George Howard undertook the management of the Troy Adelphi Theater, but the season failed and George, Caroline, and Cordelia went on the road. Howard eventually began managing a New York theater, and daughter Cordelia retired from the stage at age 13.

The city of Troy played a pivotal role in turning the Civil War in favor of the Union. Many of Troy's factories produced material for the war effort. W. & L.E. Gurley made brass fuses for bombs; Corning, Winslow & Co. made steel rifled cannons; Eaton, Gilbert & Co. made army wagons; Burden Iron Company made horseshoes; Sweet, Quimby &

Co. made shot and shells; F.W. Parmener made ammo wagons; Jones & Co. made brass cannons; and casting mortar shells were made by both Fuller, Warren and Co. and Knight, Harrison & Paine.

However, it was South Troy's iron manufacturers, the Albany Iron Works, that made machinery and plates for the Union's first ironclad warship, USS *Monitor*, a ship that changed naval history forever. Furthermore, if it wasn't for the patriotism and political connections of the owners of those iron works, John A. Griswold and John F. Winslow, the *Monitor* may never have seen the light of day.

It was the famous battle between the Federal *Monitor* and the South's *Virginia* (*Merrimac*) on the morning of March 9, 1862, at Hampton Roads, Virginia, that most historians consider the turning of the tide for the Union. The *Monitor* battled the *Virginia* to a standstill, taking away the naval advantage that the Confederacy enjoyed for a brief time.

Learning that the South was developing iron ships, the American Navy's newly created Ironclad Board placed advertisements in Northern newspapers on August 3, 1861, inviting designers to submit plans for the construction of ironclad warships. John Ericsson, a Swedish inventor who became an American citizen in 1848, wrote a letter to Abraham

John Griswold helped finance and build the hull plates for the ironclad Monitor.

The Manufacturers' Bank of Troy, located at King and River Streets in Chatham Square, financed the construction of the Monitor.

Lincoln on August 29 offering to build an ironclad vessel in 90 days. However, Ericsson, a brilliant engineer and the inventor of air compressors, boilers, engines, locomotives, naval guns, and the screw propeller, was at odds with the Navy after an accident in 1844 in which one of his cannon designs blew up, killing Secretary of the Navy T.W. Gilmer, Secretary of State Abel P. Upshur, and others.

As luck would have it, Ericsson received a visit from Cornelius Bushnell, of New Haven, Connecticut, who sought out the inventor's expertise on the matter of an ironclad ship that he was going to build called the *Galena*, parts of which were made in the Albany Iron Works. Ericsson asked Bushnell to look at a model of his *Monitor*.

Ericsson had originally submitted his design for a "cupola battery" to Emperor Napoleon III several years before during the Franco-Russian War, but it was graciously declined. Ericsson also was not new to iron ships, having designed and built them in Europe in the 1830s.

Bushnell offered to take the model and plan to Washington on the inventor's behalf and present it to the Naval Board. He presented the model to Troy's Griswold and Winslow and explained the properties of the vessel that Ericsson had given him. With their help, a letter of introduction was obtained from the governor of New York and delivered to Lincoln on Bushnell's behalf. The three men, Bushnell, Winslow, and Griswold, went to pitch the idea to the Naval Board.

The President accompanied the three men to the Navy Department, where they met with the Navy Board on September 13, 1861. It was a tough sell to the board since some Navy folks still held a grudge against Ericsson. Before Lincoln left the meeting, he had the final word that day. He was holding the model, studying its unique features, and remarked, "All I have to say is what the girl said when she stuck her foot in the stocking. It strikes me there's something in it!"

Winslow or Bushnell decided to get Ericsson to present the final case himself. He did and got the go-ahead to build the ship in 100 days. Griswold, Winslow, and Bushnell were guarantors of the project. Ericsson immediately went to work. He contracted with Thomas Fitch Rowland, proprietor of the Continental Iron Works in Greenpoint, Long Island (Brooklyn), to build the battery.

The ship was 172 feet long with a 41.5-inch beam. Two 12-inch guns were to be housed in a revolving turret. The ship would have a flat deck with only 18 inches of free board and a draft of 10 feet, 6 inches. This would allow the ship to easily operate and maneuver in any of the South's inland waters.

The Monitor's *officers pose on deck in Virginia, 1862. Seated at bottom left is Third Assistant Engineer Robinson W. Hands, a Troy native who drowned when the ironclad sank.*

The majority of the iron plates, bolts, nuts, and rivets were manufactured in New York State. Holdane & Company, the Albany Iron Works, and the Rensselaer Iron Works provided tons of flat plates and angle iron. The Niagara Steam Forge pounded out the 8-inch-thick port stoppers. The turret and machinery were made at the Novelty Iron Works.

Back in the early 1980s, workers at the old Iron Works (then called Portec) exhibited a few extra *Monitor* hull plates that they had in storage and which are now in the possession of the Mohawk Hudson Gateway's Burden Museum.

The iron turret had an interior diameter of 20 feet. The eight layers of 1-inch-thick plate were assembled around an iron skeleton. The structure was powered by two "donkey engines," which turned massive gears and provided the turret with 2.5 r.p.m. The turret revolved on a brass ring set into the deck, and a shaft from below raised up by a wedge and set to put the turret in motion. When Ericsson learned that the Navy had no 12-inch guns ready, he recalculated to incorporate two 11-inch Dahlgren smoothbore cannons. The public was not impressed. Local papers began printing articles about "Ericsson's Folly" and how the ship would slide to the bottom of the East River when launched.

On January 20, 1862, Ericsson wrote to Secretary Fox proposing that the name of the ship be the *Monitor*. Ten days later, on January 30, 1862, 101 days after the contract was signed, a ship that was unlike anything the world had seen slid down into the East River at the Continental Iron Works. There were many bystanders who were witness to what they thought would be a disaster. Ericsson stood on the stern of his ship, and when launched, it floated to within 3 inches of his designed water line.

This painting depicts the loss of the Monitor *in 1862.*

The ship was turned over to the Navy Department and commissioned on February 25, 1862. It had devices containing more than 40 original patents on board, including a flush toilet. The USS *Monitor* steamed for Hampton Roads in Virginia on March 6, 1862, and on the morning of March 9, 1862, entered the annals of history forever.

During the Civil War, the Union began the building of 76 ironclad war ships, commissioning 42 of them before May 1, 1865. On the Confederate side, 59 ironclads were started, but only 24 were completed. Very few Civil War ironclads were sunk by gunfire. Instead, the Confederate ironclads were purposely destroyed to prevent capture by Union forces. Of the total of 66 ironclads on both sides combined, only 12 were actually sunk by the enemy in battle. However, none of them developed a legend like the battle between the Union's *Monitor* and the Confederacy's *Virginia* (*Merrimac*).

On the afternoon of March 8, 1862, a naval battle occurred that changed naval warfare forever. The first Confederate ironclad steamed down the Elizabeth River into Hampton Roads, Virginia, to attack the wood-sided Federal blockading fleet anchored there. The CSS *Virginia*, or *Merrimac*, was originally a wooden ship sunk by the Union, but it was raised by Confederate engineers and converted into an ironclad ship. This vessel attacked the Union Navy fleet, comprising several ships armed with 204 guns and aided by land batteries.

By six o'clock, the sole *Virginia* had sunk the *Cumberland*, burned the *Congress*, forced the *Minnesota* ashore, and forced the *St. Lawrence* and the *Roanoke* to seek shelter under the guns of Fort Monroe. The rebel ship left the Union fleet in shambles with plans to return the next day to finish the job. The results of the first day's fighting at Hampton Roads proved the superiority of iron over wood, but on the next day, it was to be iron versus iron, as the USS *Monitor* arrived on the scene.

On March 9, the *Virginia* was greeted by the *Monitor*, an ironclad more heavily armored, with a revolving gun turret, and speedier and more agile in the water due to the inventive genius of its designer, John Ericsson.

For four to five hours, the two ironclads battered each other, until a shell from the *Virginia* exploded on the eyeslit of the *Monitor's* pilot house, blinding the commander, Captain John L. Worden. Both ships withdrew thinking they had won.

Lieutenant S. Dana Greene, an officer aboard the *Monitor*, described the first exchange of gunfire with the following: "The turrets and other parts of the ship were heavily struck, but the shots did not penetrate; the tower was intact, and it continued to revolve. A look of confidence passed over the men's faces, and we believed the *Merrimac* [CSS *Virginia*] would not repeat the work she had accomplished the day before." The next day, the following information was sent in a letter to Major General George McClellan, commander of the Federal forces, from Major General John E. Wool, commander of Fort Monroe: "General: Two hours after I sent my hurried dispatch to the Secretary of War last evening the *Monitor* arrived, and saved the *Minnesota* and the *St. Lawrence*, which were both aground when she arrived." Wool, a hero of two previous wars, and also from Troy, fired off another letter to his friend John Griswold and wrote, "The *Monitor* saved everything inside and outside Fortress Monroe." Clearly both Trojans knew that they had a hand in preventing the further destruction of the Union Navy, clearly giving the strategic victory to the North.

During the night of the battle at Hampton Roads, ironworkers who helped make the plates for the *Monitor* marched by torchlight to downtown Troy in celebration. Today, several of the hull plates rolled but not used are on display at the Burden Iron Works Museum in the Burden Office Building, operated by the Hudson Mohawk Industrial Gateway in South Troy. The bank room where the finances were developed in the old Manufacturers National Bank of Troy was removed when the old building was demolished on the corner of King and River and reassembled into their new bank building on the corner of Grand and Fourth. The room is still there to view. Wool's quote to Griswold and a scene of the famous battle are depicted on the statue at Monument Square. Trojan iron magnates John A. Griswold and John F. Winslow made a major contribution to the Civil War.

There are many firsts associated with the USS *Monitor*. It was the first ship to have a revolving turret. It was the first ship where the officers and crew had to live entirely below the waterline, and it was the first ship credited with having below-waterline flushing toilets. Finally, the *Monitor* and its grave site is the first U.S. National Marine Sanctuary.

Lieutenant Samuel Dana Greene, executive officer on the *Monitor*, wrote a series of articles on the Battle of Hampton Roads and described the *Monitor*'s fatal night on December 31, 1862, when she was sunk by a storm:

> With the withdrawal of McClellan's army, we returned to Hampton Roads, and in the autumn were ordered to Washington, where the vessel was repaired. We returned to Hampton Roads in November, and sailed thence [December 29] in tow of the steamer *Rhode Island*, bound for Beaufort, N.C. Between 11 p.m. and midnight on the following night the *Monitor* went down in a gale, a few miles south of Cape Hatteras. Four officers and twelve men were drowned, forty-nine people being saved by the boats of the steamer. It was impossible to keep the vessel free of water, and we presumed that the upper and lower hulls thumped themselves apart.

One of those officers who went down with the *Monitor* was Trojan Robinson Woollen Hands (1838–1862), who served on the *Monitor* as third assistant engineer. He is buried in the new Mount Ida Cemetery off Pawling Avenue. His headstone reads, "Born at Sea Died at Sea."

12. Getting Around

Traveling across imposing geographical restraints like rivers or forests was not very convenient for those living in Troy two centuries ago. It took hours or days to get anywhere, and if the voyager wanted a half-way pleasurable trip, it normally cost a toll. Luxury was not part of the deal either. The principal ways to travel during Troy's first hundred years were with horses, wagons, stagecoaches, steamboats, trolleys, and railroads.

Those who wanted to cross the river took the ferry, powered by men, horses, and later (1826) steam, or for those longer journeys, a trip on the steamboats that plied the waters between New York City and Troy. Traveling over land meant pay-by-the-mile toll roads that were often full of ruts, and if the traveler was not taking his/her own horse or buggy, the stagecoach ride was not the ride of a Lincoln. It was not until 1835 that a railroad carried passengers to Troy, and not until 1861, when horse-drawn, and later electric, trolleys made traveling more pleasant.

For the very early settlers of the region, a ferryboat, owned by the Vanderheyden family, plied the waters between Ferry Street and Stony Point (Watervliet) in 1707. Troy was known in those days as Vanderheyden's Ferry, or Ferry Hook in 1786. When Captain Stephen Ashley leased the ferry operation from Vanderheyden, it became known as Ashley's Ferry. For a few pennies, a person could take a wagon and horses across the river, boarding when he or she heard the blowing of a conch shell a few minutes before leaving. References to the ferry ceased when the newly created village was named Vanderheyden and later Troy in 1789. However, by the late nineteenth century, there were four ferries crossing the river at Troy. A Supreme Court decision took away the exclusive ferry rights of the Vanderheyden heirs in 1854.

In 1798, Mahlon Taylor created a ferry service in the south part of Troy at Washington Street. The ferries were large flat-bottom boats propelled by iron-pointed poles. Historian Arthur Weise stated that they were later attached to ropes stretched across the river. Taylor's ferry took off at the landing near the Clinton Stove Works and landed at a point where the Watervliet Arsenal is now located. In 1809, Moses Crafts received a patent for his invention of propelling boats using horse power.

A ferry was established at the foot of Broadway, landing on the south end of Green Island. On October 13, 1854, a ferry sunk and 11 passengers drowned. Apparently, the passengers stood to prevent the swells from the steamboat *Alice* from getting in the boat and capsized the boat. The fourth ferry was located at Douw Street, landing at the foot of Tibbits Street in Green Island. In 1911, a ferry went over the dam, killing three people.

While these early ferries were successful, enterprising Trojans began the construction of two major overland turnpikes—the Northern Turnpike to Vermont and the Troy-Schenectady Turnpike to Schenectady. The 50-mile Northern Turnpike began, in 1799, at the corner of 124th Street and Fourth Avenue in Lansingburgh and ended at the line in Rupert, Vermont. The 16-mile Troy-Schenectady Turnpike (now Route 7, Troy-Schenectady Road) was built in 1802 and was designed to funnel trade from the Mohawk Valley to Troy instead of Albany. Both of these were toll roads.

Later roads were laid with planks to make it easier for travelers. One of the earliest was the Troy and Berlin Turnpike in 1840. Part of Fifth Avenue in the Burgh was a plank road. These plank and toll roads were welcome by stagecoach lines.

In 1786, a stagecoach route began at the Phoenix Hotel in Lansingburgh and went to Troy and later to Albany. A stage between Troy and Schenectady made its first trip on May 5, 1823. A stagecoach trip from Troy to Albany took two hours; in 1846, a stage to Montreal, Canada took four days.

The Congress Street bridge was the second-largest highway bridge in the United States when it was built in 1872.

For those travelers who didn't like the ferries or coaches, they could take a walk or ride over a bridge beginning in the nineteenth century. The first bridge to span the Hudson actually was built in Lansingburgh. The Union Bridge, constructed in 1804, was the first bridge to span the Hudson River, connecting Waterford to Lansingburgh, and it was located at the site of the present bridge. At a cost of $20,000, the bridge was declared an engineering feat. Large hewn timbers squared by hand axes were pinioned together with large wooden pegs and iron strips welded together. When the bridge burned in 1909, it was the oldest covered bridge in America. While the original bridge was built for trolleys and was toll based, a newer iron bridge with fireproof floors took its place and was toll free. This covered bridge was 800 feet long and 30 feet wide. Horses and wagons (later trolleys) drove through the center and pedestrian walkways flanked each side.

The Rensselaer and Saratoga Railroad Company tried to lease the bridge but residents in Lansingburgh declined, so the company built its own wooden covered bridge in 1834 on eight stone piers that spanned 1,600 feet from Chatham Square in downtown Troy to Green Island (where the present Green Island Bridge sits). This bridge was the first between New York City and Waterford. The first passenger cars ran over the bridge on October 6, 1835. It also had a carriage road and footway and there was a toll charge. This bridge burned in 1862, taking most of Troy's business district with it. A new iron bridge was built in 1876 and 1884—it too charged tolls. The eastern end fell into the river in 1977 and was replaced with a new, Art Deco–style span.

In 1872, the second Troy bridge was built at the foot of Congress Street at a cost of $350,000 by the Troy and West Troy Bridge Company. It was paid for by tolls. The second largest highway bridge in America, it was featured in *Scientific American* magazine. The bridge was replaced in 1915–1917 by a newer electrically controlled drawbridge and became toll free. New York's Department of Transportation had to blow up this bridge in 1971 to replace it with the present span.

In 1880, Cohoes was connected to Lansingburgh by a toll bridge, but it was replaced by an iron bridge with wood floors. This burned in 1920 and was replaced by a concrete bridge in 1923. Before the new bridge was erected, a hanging walkway was constructed over the river. Old timers called it the "Swing," as it rocked back and forth in the wind.

The last historic bridge was the Menands Bridge, built in 1933, connecting South Troy to Menands. The towers have recently been taken down and there are plans to remove this bridge for a new one.

THE STEAMBOAT ERA

On September 4, 1807, a small steamboat named the *North River Steamboat* set out on its maiden voyage from New York City and reached Albany the following morning. It was the beginning of the steamboat era that would capture a traveling population for over a century. Robert R. Livingston and Robert Fulton were granted a 30-year "privilege" to use their boats to carry people and freight on the river. The first such boat was the *FireFly*, which began transporting people between Albany and Troy in September 1812. For 2 shillings, one could travel each way, or rent the ship for a 3-hour evening excursion for $4. However, Chief Justice John Marshall of the Supreme Court ruled this privilege unconstitutional on May 2, 1824, and opened the door for a number of steamboat companies to form almost overnight.

Trojans didn't waste any time and immediately created the Troy Steamboat Company on March 31, 1825. Troy's first steamboat, appropriately named the *Chief Justice Marshall*, arrived at the Ferry Street dock the following March. Shortly after, the *Constitution* and *Constellation* began regular trips between Troy and New York City. In 1826, the first "day" boat, the *New London*, began the voyage to the city. By 1844, 8 steamboats, 10 steamboat tows, 24 freight barges, and 27 sailing vessels, all owned by Trojans, were in the business of carrying freight and passengers.

By 1871, the Citizen's Steamboat Company was organized by Joseph Cornell, George W. Horton, and Captain Thomas Abrams, supported by local subscriptions, for a night line between Troy and New York City. After purchasing several boats, such as the *Thomas Powell*, *Sunnyside*, *C. Vanderbilt*, and *Connecticut*, the firm launched the impressive *City of Troy* (1876), a 300-foot-long steamboat with 112 state rooms and 250 separate rooms for men and women, and the *Saratoga* (1877), also 300 feet long with 113 state rooms and 250 rooms for men and women.

Boarding the steamboats in Troy took place either at the State Street landing or Broadway landing (earlier boats launched at Ferry). Passengers boarded the first by going through the ticket office at River and walking through and over a long covered platform to the boat. On Broadway, a covered shed kept passengers out of the elements. A daily trip took 10 hours.

Between 1809 and 1876, 72 different steamboats went up and down the river between Troy and New York City.

Albany steamboat companies such as the Hudson Navigation Company also had their boats ply between Troy, Albany, and New York. Trojans boarded the *Trojan* or *Rensselaer* nightly. In fact, Albany "day" boats continued running into the 1960s. In 1962, the Albany Day Line was purchased by Francis J. Barry.

The *Alexander Hamilton* was continued in service by Day Line, Inc., a subsidiary of Barry, and was in operation until 1971, retiring at the ripe age of 47. Designed by J.W. Millard & Brother, it was built for $750,000 in 1923–1924 by the Sparrows Point plant of the Bethlehem Shipbuilding Company (348 feet length, 76 feet extreme beam, and 13.8 feet depth of hold).

The *Peter Stuyvesant*, another old day boat, became part of the Anthony's Pier 4 restaurant in Boston. Most of the other boats were sold and scrapped. The design of the Lake George boat *Saint Sacrament* was based on this old steamer. The Albany Night Line had several giants in its service—the *Adirondack*, the *C.W. Morse*, and the *Berkshire*, the largest river steamboat ever built in the world.

TROY'S TROLLEY

It was 1860 when the Troy and Lansingburgh Horse Railway was created by a few enterprising Trojans who saw that stagecoaches were not able to keep up with a growing population. On July 31, 1860, the Common Council gave this new company permission to lay a single track down River, Adam, and Second Streets to a point near where the South

End Tavern exists today. On August 30, 1861, the first horse-drawn trolley car went over the route. Low in height, broad, and roomy, it was painted red, like the other five that would make up the fleet that became known as the "Red" line. The line was extended to Waterford in 1862. During the month of November, 80 daily trips were made on this small route, which totaled 6.5 miles from Waterford to the Wyantskill.

The Troy and Cohoes Horse Car Railroad, called the "White" line, followed on February 11, 1862, and made the first trip on October 10, 1863. It went from the east side of the Rensselaer and Saratoga Bridge (today's Green Island Bridge) through Green Island to the Champlain Canal at Cohoes and to Ferry Street in Troy.

Organized in January 1866, the Troy and Albia Horse Railroad Company went from the center of Troy 3.5 miles up to Albia. This was followed by the "Blue" line, where Cohoes connected to Lansingburgh in 1880 via Ontario Street, Simmons, and VanSchaick Islands, intersecting with the Lansingburgh-Troy line near 112th Street. A line connecting Cohoes to Waterford began in 1884 and was known as the "Green" line.

The Troy and Lansingburgh Railway increased its reach throughout the city and by 1886 employed 206 men employed, and owned 95 cars and 468 horses. Car barns were located in both ends of the city. According to historian Rutherford Hayner, more than 5,000 people rode the horse railroads in 1885.

On September 29, 1889, the northern part of the Troy-Lansingburgh road from 101st Street to the Waterford Bridge was electrified using the Sprague Single Overhead Wire System. The horse trolley had seen its day. The street railway companies then merged

Launched on April 1, 1876, the City of Troy arrived at the steamboat landing at Broadway on June 15. Owned by the Citizen's Steamboat Company of Troy, organized in 1871, the steamer was 300 feet in length, 70 feet in breadth, and weighed 1,650 tons. It had 112 state rooms, 40 ladies cabin berths, and 210 berths for men. It took 10 hours to travel from Troy to New York City, making daily trips (except on Saturdays). The City of Troy burned on April 5, 1907, 31 years after it was launched.

under the Troy City Railway system. In 1900, the trolley lines of Troy, Albany, and the surrounding areas merged into the United Traction Company. By now, over 100 miles of territory were covered by trolleys and interurbans (trolleys that went between cities).

Only six years later, the Delaware & Hudson Company (D&H) purchased United Traction. If you can't beat them, buy them. The D&H did not like the fact that the extensive trolley system was competing with their intercity routes. The D&H and New York Central developed an Albany-Troy "Belt Line" with 30 trains traveling each weekday between Albany and Troy and the suburbs only 25 minutes apart.

The writing on the wall for the trolleys came in October 1924 when a trackless trolley was demonstrated in Troy. Buses would soon kill off the trolley—after all they were not confined to restrictive and costly tracks. Even Lansingburgh got its own bus system, the Fifth Avenue Bus Company, in 1915.

While it seems romantic riding the trolley cars, one old-time Trojan, Mal Hormats, explained that the rides could get somewhat out of hand. As a kid, he used to commute on the old Hoosick Street trolley at 5¢ a pop. In 1933, one trolley got away from the motorman and hit the building on the southwest corner of Hoosick and River. The motorman was killed, the trolley smashed, but hardly a brick was chipped on the building.

TROY'S RAILROADS

Most Trojans growing up in the city have a special fascination with railroads since trains ran right through the heart of the city several times a day until the late 1950s. All but a few reminders of Troy's glorious railroad history survive. Most of it has been destroyed and taken away.

The block around Union, Broadway, Fulton, and Sixth Avenue was Troy's railroad hub in the form of the Union Railroad Station. Union Station was built in 1854, and burned in the great fire of 1862, but was immediately rebuilt. In 1903, a new Beaux Arts–style station took its place and lasted until 1958, when it was replaced by a parking lot. The station was controlled by the Rensselaer & Saratoga (1835), Troy & Schenectady (1842), Troy & Greenbush (1845), and Troy & Boston (1852) Railroads. Later, these companies were consolidated by the New York Central and Boston & Maine Railroads.

Trains entered Troy from Rensselaer, Green Island, and from the north. They crossed into the city in South Troy starting at Madison and headed northeast until reaching the Market Block at Liberty. From there the trains went into a small tunnel under Fifth Avenue, then hugged Mount Ida until they went through the Ferry Street Tunnel, exiting at Congress, and reaching the station a few feet from there. Trains also rumbled over the Green Island Bridge with the tracks splitting south into the train station, or north to the rail yards at Middleburgh Street and beyond. Still visible are the track right-a-ways past the bridge at a set of angled buildings along Fifth Avenue and Grand Street.

Motorists had to wait for the trains to cross the street since the trains had the right of way. Every street and alley crossed by a train had a small shanty and a railroad man who would come out and stand in the street with a large sign pole. Sometimes, long trains near the station would be backed up blocking Broadway. Pedestrians simply climbed up and through the cars to the other side.

The Albia #294 of the Troy Railway trolley is ready for action. All of the trolley systems in Troy merged on September 29, 1889 to form the Troy City Railway.

The train station was a block long and the interior had a large central hall with a grand ceiling and huge windows. The ticket window was to the west (Union Street). To enter the trains, passengers exited through doors on the east; a large clock above told the departure times. For those headed north, a climb down a pair of stairs took them into a subway tunnel that looked like a Greek temple and exited on the other side of Sixth Avenue. Outside, passengers were shielded from the elements by a long, overhanging platform.

Troy's rail days were impressive. In the early teens, there were 130 passenger trains a day (1 every 11 minutes) going through the city. There were more than 30 trains running daily between Troy and Albany, 25 minutes apart on the commuter "Beltway."

None of Troy's early transportation infrastructure survives today. All but the most recent historic Menands Bridge (1933) have been replaced by bridges such as the Congress Street Bridge, the Collar City Bridge, and the Ferry Street Bridge. Troy's trolley car tracks are buried beneath the asphalt-paved streets, and all the train tracks through the city have been ripped up. Finally, the age of steamboats has no vestiges along the riverbanks. Sadly, the City is trying to accommodate the car culture by building parking garages and turning vacant building lots into parking lots. Mass transportation, what exists in the form of taxis and buses, tries to help out the few car-less residents. Whether Troy will ever become a transportation hub again is anyone's guess.

13. Leisure Times

Troy has a long history in arts and entertainment, going back to the days before the city was even incorporated. Entertainment, however, comes in many forms. On May 20, 1793, at Ashley's Tavern on Ferry Street, a Mr. Moore entertained with a series of lectures, apparently a set of humorous remarks, for an admission of 2 shillings and 6 pence for adults (kids cost 1 shilling and 6 pence). A few years later, in October 1800, an African lion was exhibited for a few days. On October 8, 1805, a live elephant was exhibited at Moulton's Coffee House (where Russell Sage is now) also for a short period. These were considered exotic animals of course and created quite an interest.

Musical contributions were recorded as early as 1822 at Babcock's Hotel on River Street. Somewhere in between an exhibit of a dwarf cow and an educated bear that could read, spell, subtract, multiply, and divide, was music on King David's cymbal, an ancient instrument, and music on the leaf, accompanied by violin and organ. A year later, a Mr. Keene gave a vocal concert along with the piano.

On Fifth Avenue and Ferry Street at Mr. Churchill's Store room, one heard the theatrical performance of Mr. and Mrs. Russell and their daughter, whose moral plays required only 25¢ admission. Front seats were for ladies only.

As early as 1829, Troy's Public Markets offered drama. Patrons got their meat on the first floor and entertainment on the second. The second floor of the North Market on Federal was opened on July 4 with a play called *Pizarro, or the Death of Rollo*. In February 1847, the hall on the second floor of Fulton Market, at the corner of Fulton and River, opened with the play *The Lady of Lyons*.

In late September 1836, when workers were excavating for Mill No. 3 of the Harmony Mills in Cohoes, the bones of a prehistoric mastodont were found embedded in peat in two potholes. These fossils were put on display in Harmony Hall at the corner of River and Third Streets for a duration before they were donated to the New York State Museum in Albany. Across the street at the Peale Troy Museum, *Uncle Tom's Cabin* was first performed in the United States in 1852.

Troy's Knockout Boys

Boxing has been around for a very long time. There is evidence of fist-fighting as a sport in Ethiopia about 6,000 years ago. It eventually spread to Egypt and throughout the

Mediterranean region. Even ancient Crete had a boxing-like sport around 1,500 B.C. In Greece, two boxers sat on stones facing each other and pounded away until one of them was knocked out. Fighters did wear leather thongs to protect their hands and wrists, but as it progressed, these thongs turned into weapons as harder leather was used. There were no breaks in the fighting either. The Greeks introduced the sport into the Olympic games, complete with rules, back in 688 B.C. However, the Olympics were also performed in the nude, so better to have rules than not.

The Roman Empire continued the boxing tradition, sort of, and invented the boxing ring, a circle drawn in the sand or platform—hence, today's square boxing platform is called a "ring." The Roman form of the sport was more like their gladiator events, often brutal in comparison to the Greeks. They created the *Caestus*, a leather wrapping with iron and brass studs obviously designed to inflict pain. Apparently that wasn't painful enough for them so they created the bronze *Myrmex* (which means "limb piercer"). Since they were using slaves to fight the contests, it was more like a TV special—a fight to the death entertainment show—than boxing as we know it today. Rome eventually banned the limb piercer and boxing altogether around 30 B.C.

After Rome fell, it would take more than 1,000 years before the sport was reintroduced by the English. It was an illiterate Englishmen, James Figg, the first heavyweight

John Morrissey won the heavyweight championship of America in 1853 against Yankee Sullivan.

champion in the sport's history, who opened a fight academy in London in 1719, and made boxing popular (he was also a fencer, so was "respectable"). Yet, it took another 24 years before the well-educated Jack Broughton, considered the "Father of English Boxing," wrote the first British boxing rules. These rules outlawed hitting below the belt or hitting an opponent that was down. Wrestling holds were allowed but only above the waist. Under Broughton's rules, there was a 3-foot square in the center of the ring and when a fighter was knocked down, his handlers had 30 seconds to pick him up and position him on one side of the square, or the fight was over. Broughton is given credit for inventing the first boxing gloves, called "mufflers," but they were used only in practice, not in real fights.

These rules were used throughout England with only minor tampering until the Pugilistic Society, founded in 1814, developed the London Prize Ring Rules in 1838. The new rules called for a ring 24 feet square, enclosed by two ropes. A knockdown marked the end of a round. Rounds were introduced with a 30-second break. The fighters were given 8 seconds to "toe the mark," or "come to scratch," unaided, in the center of the ring after the break or the fight was over. English rules were used until 1889, when the last bare-knuckle championship bout was fought.

Paddy Ryan, seen here in 1884, won the first true heavyweight championship of the world against Joe Goss, the English champion, in 1880.

Boxing first began in America between black slaves whose masters wagered huge sums against them. The first great American fighter, a slave named Tom Molineaux, won his freedom by knocking out a champ from a rival plantation. In 1809, he went to England to fight and won a couple, and in 1810–1811, he fought and lost to the English champion, Tom Crib. His jaw was broken in the last fight.

Bill Richmond, the "Black Terror" of Staten Island, was a servant of General Lord Percy, who commanded the British forces occupying New York during the Revolution. Richmond fought a number of British soldiers and never lost. Percy took him to England to fight in 1777. At age 41, Richmond knocked out his first English opponent in 25 seconds. In 1805, he, too, was knocked out by British champion Tom Cribb. Richmond continued fighting until he was 52 and never lost again.

Most fighting in America was frowned upon and even made illegal in the eastern part of the country, so many fights were held in the Midwest to escape the law. It wasn't until after the Civil War that boxing came into its own. Credit is given to the Boston boxer John L. Sullivan and the Queensbury Rules for making the sport popular and acceptable here.

In 1866, the Marquis of Queensbury, a big supporter in British sporting circles, laid down a new set of rules. These rules included the mandatory wearing of gloves. Unlike the English rules that dealt with bare knuckle, there was no wrestling allowed at all. Rounds were 3 minutes with a 1 minute rest period in between. Finally, a boxer had 10 seconds to recover from a knockdown. These are the basic rules we follow today.

John L. Sullivan (1858–1918), the "Boston Strong Boy," became the first great sports hero in America and began his rise in fame by beating Troy's Paddy Ryan, which is known in boxing circles as the first great prize fight in American boxing history. Sullivan was known as an honest fighter. He would fight anyone (but refused to fight black men), anywhere, with bare fists, skin-tight or padded gloves, and under any rules. He is credited with saying, "I will fight any man breathing. Always on the level, yours truly, John L. Sullivan."

Troy has a unique place in the early history of American boxing with three fighters: Paddy Ryan, John Morrissey, and John C. Heenan. All three were bare-knuckle fighters and two of them, Ryan and Morrissey, were heavyweight champions of America.

For the working class, living in Troy during the nineteenth century often meant using your fists to get by. The infamous "Watervliet Cut," a lateral part of the Erie Canal that allowed access to Troy, was lined with saloons, and one writer reported that bodies were found floating in that portion of the canal way too often. Troy's first boxing champion ran one of those saloons. Patrick Henry "Paddy" Ryan (1851–1900), known as the Trojan Giant, was born in Thurles, Tipperary, Ireland, on March 14, 1851, but lived in Troy, West Troy, and Green Island most of his life. Standing at 5 feet, 11 inches (some reports are 6 feet, 1.5 inches), he weighed in at 195–200 pounds. According to some reports, Ryan was a better wrestler than a boxer, but he certainly did like to fight. He opened his famous saloon at the Sidecut around 1874. His ease at dealing with "problems" impressed Jimmy Killoran, athletic director at the Rensselaer Polytechnic Institute. Taking Ryan under his wing, Ryan was ready for professional boxing by 1877.

On May 30, 1880, Paddy won the first true Heavyweight Championship of the World from Joe Goss, the English champion, at Coillier's Station, West Virginia, in the 87th round (after fighting an hour and a half). Paddy lost it two years later, on February 7, fighting John L. Sullivan, the Boston Strong Boy (bare knuckled and under London Prize Ring rules) in nine rounds. Ryan reportedly said that Sullivan, a powerful right-handed puncher, "hit me like he held a telegraph pole." Ryan and Sullivan liked to fight each other. Between January 19, 1885, and February 17, 1897, Sullivan fought Paddy at least a dozen times—with Sullivan winning all the matches.

Ryan died on December 14, 1900, in a rented house on Albany Avenue, Green Island, and was buried in St. Mary's Cemetery in that village. He was elected to the Ring Boxing Hall of Fame in 1973.

John Morrissey (1831–1878), known as "Old Smoke," was born in Templemore, Tipperary County, Ireland, on February 5, 1831, but was raised by an immigrant Irish family in Troy. He stood close to 6 feet tall and weighed in at 170–176 pounds.

Morrissey got his nickname "Old Smoke" from a battle against a Native American named Tom McCann. Morrissey was pinned on his back over burning coals from a stove that had been knocked over in the bout. While steam and smoke and the smell of burning flesh permeated from Morrissey, he continued to fight without notice. This came as a surprise to the crowd that expected him to call "Enough," the signal to surrender.

Morrissey didn't have many fights, but he did win the Heavyweight Championship of America on October 12, 1853, at Boston Corners, New York, on the border of Massachusetts and New York, against Yankee Sullivan (James Ambrose, alias Frank Murray). Sullivan apparently won the fight and beat Morrissey badly, but left the ring and ignored the "time" call, so the referee declared Morrissey the winner.

Morrissey upheld his heavyweight title against Troy's John C. Heenan on October 20, 1858, at Long Point, Canada. Heenan actually broke his right hand early on in the fight and fought at a disadvantage. Morrissey gave up the heavyweight championship and retired from the ring.

Morrissey was known as a strong, tough fighter but had little boxing acumen. After retiring from the ring, he became a prominent politician and served two terms in the U.S. Congress and twice in the New York State Senate. He is probably better known for creating the Saratoga Racetrack. Morrissey opened gambling operations in Saratoga for the summer spa season in the 1860s and opened his soon-to-become world-famous Clubhouse in 1870. He began the horseracing course in the late 1860s. Morrissey was a pioneer in using the newly invented telegraph to make betting available to everyone.

The ex-boxer died on May 1, 1878, at the Adelphi Hotel in Saratoga at age 47 and was buried in Saratoga. He had just won an election against Tammany Hall's hand-picked candidate in the wealthiest election district in New York City. The New York State Legislature closed on the day of his burial, and the entire elected body attended funeral services in Troy. An estimated crowd of 12,000 stood outside the church to pay tribute to the American champion. He was elected to the Ring Boxing Hall of Fame in 1954.

John Camel Heenan (1835–1873) was the only one of the three actually born in Troy. Born on May 2, 1835, he was raised by an immigrant Irish family also. Heenan stood 6 feet 2 inches and weighed in at 182–195 pounds. He was known as the Benicia Boy, from swinging a sledgehammer in the Pacific Mail Steamship Company's Benicia, California repair works. Heenan fought John Morrissey for the Heavyweight Championship of

America in 1858, but broke his right hand early in the fight hitting a ring stake and fought at a disadvantage.

Heenan was the first American boxer known to lift weights and punch bags as part of his training regimen for a bout with the English champion Thomas Sayers. On April 17, 1860, in Hampshire, England, Heenan fought the 5-foot, 8-inch, 154-pound Sayers. Sayers fractured his right arm in the sixth round from a hit by Heenan. Constables tried to stop the fight in the 36th round after two hours, but spectators were pushed into the ring. They fought five more rounds before it was finally declared a draw. Champion belts were made for both fighters.

Heenan was known as a clever boxer with "tremendous punching power," but was probably better known for marrying Adah Isaacs Menken, a famous San Francisco actress of the time who played the notorious, glamorous, and beautiful "Mazeppa," a title character based on the poem of Lord Byron. Heenan made a practice of beating Adah every night after dinner, so she divorced him. She married five times. Heenan toured around the country with Englishman "Gypsy" Jem Mace, the "Father of Modern Boxing," giving exhibitions. He died at Green River Station, Wyoming Territory, on November 2, 1873, and was buried in St. Agnus Cemetery in Menands. The Benicia Boy was elected to the Ring Boxing Hall of Fame in 1954.

John C. Heenan, the "Benicia Boy," was elected to the Ring Boxing Hall of Fame in 1954.

In the twentieth century, the Troy area continued to be an important place in boxing circles. Few know that boxer Mike Tyson had his first 15 bouts under the leadership of Troy's Uncle Sam Boxing Club with Bob and Lorraine Miller. The records show that his first Troy bout was on February 16, 1986, with Jesse Ferguson, a fight that Tyson won with a KO in the sixth round. He also fought in Troy again on June 28 with William Hosea (KO in the first). Tyson went on to become the youngest heavyweight in history.

The Troy area had other fighters. In more recent times, Dave "Ziggy" Zyglewicz fought Joe Frazier on April 22, 1969, in Houston, Texas (and lost in first round). How many remember Ted Bailey's outdoor boxing ring in South Troy? The boxing tradition continues in the Troy area more recently with Danny Ferris, Danny Chapman, and Timmy Lavalley.

TROY'S NATIONAL LEAGUE DAYS

It was more than 150 years ago that the first organized baseball game was played at Elysian Fields in Hoboken, New Jersey, on June 19, 1846. The New York Base Ball Club defeated Alexander Cartwright's New York Knickerbockers 23-1 in four innings. By the mid- to late 1850s, places like Buffalo, Syracuse, Albany, and Troy all had local baseball teams. By 1856, ten years after it was introduced by Alexander Cartwright, not Abner Doubleday, the *New York Clipper* announced on December 15 that "the game of Base Ball is generally considered the National game amongst Americans."

The Haymakers team poses for a portrait, with two players holding hay rakes.

On January 10, 1857, the first of several "leagues" was formed—the National Association of Base Ball Players. By 1860, 62 teams, including the Victorys of Troy, were members. The next year saw Troy combining two teams, the Priams of Troy and the National Club of Lansingburgh, into the Unions of Rensselaer County. This team was short lived and folded at the outbreak of the Civil War.

In 1866, after the war, the team reorganized as the Unions of Lansingburgh and played most of their games at Rensselaer Park (between 108th and 110th Streets) for five seasons. A bleacher was built especially for the team in the middle of the park's racetrack. During those five seasons, the Unions won most of their games. During a game between the Unions and New York Mutuals in 1867, in which the Unions won, one of the Mutuals' players expressed his disbelief at losing to a bunch of Upstate "haymakers." The Haymakers name stuck.

On March 17, 1871, another league, the National Association of Professional Base Ball Players, was formed in New York City. Nine teams, including the now "Troy Haymakers," paid the $10 membership fee. This team, however, lasted less than two years. Not able to pay its players, or its bills, the team dissolved on July 24, 1872.

Troy baseball was not dead yet. On February 2, 1876, yet another league was organized at New York City's Grand Central Hotel—the National League of Professional Base Ball Clubs (present-day National League). Three years later, on January 26, 1879, the Lansingburgh Haymakers were granted National League membership and changed their name to the Troy Trojans (also known as the Troy Cities). The Trojans did not fare well. Their 1879 debut season placed them in the cellar with a 19-56 record, 35.5 games behind the first-place Providence Grays. The next year, they finished in fourth place with a 41-42 record. The 1881 season had them 39-45, in fifth place. Finally, in 1882, their last year, they came in seventh place with a record of 35-48. In total, they won 134 games and lost 191.

However, the Trojans did set a record that has never been broken. On September 22, 1881, the Trojans set an attendance record in a rain-drenched game against the Chicago White Stockings. Only 12 fans showed up. The Trojans beat the White Stockings 10-8.

The year 1882 was the last for professional baseball in Troy. The newly formed American Association (League) was giving the National League a run for the money. The National League decided to throw out its small-market clubs—Troy and Worcester, Massachusetts. The Trojans ended the 1882 season by beating Worcester, 10-7. This was the last National League game played in Troy.

On December 6, 1882, at the National League's annual convention, the Troy Trojans and Worcester Brown Stockings were cut from the league in a 6-2 vote. However, to take out the sting, both Troy and Worcester were granted honorary membership in the National League. To this day, Troy is an honorary member of the National League.

The Trojans were disbanded after the 1882 season, but New York tobacco tycoon John Day bought the rights to the Trojans and shipped many of the players to his New York Metropolitans of the American Association, and the Gothams (Giants) of the National League. The San Francisco Giants, with their roots here in Troy, continue to play today.

Of the 76 or so ball players that made up the various teams of the Troy Haymakers between 1866 and 1882, a handful of them rose above the rest. While the Troy team was in the National League for a short four years, it produced five players that had careers that landed them in the Hall of Fame in Cooperstown.

"Big Dan" Brouthers (1858–1932) joined Troy in 1879, but was sent back to the minors for making too many errors and ended up playing for a number of teams (he even tried pitching for Troy). He ended up leading the league in batting average in 1882–1883, 1889, 1891–1892; in home runs in 1881 and 1886; and in RBIs in 1892. In 1881, he was sent to Buffalo, where he led the league in homers (8) and batted .368 in 1882 and .374 in 1883. On September 10, 1886, he hit three home runs, a double, and a single for 15 total bases.

Brouthers won the batting title (.373) in 1889 for the Boston Beaneaters. In 1891, he joined the pennant-winning Boston Reds of the American Association and won the batting title with a .350 average. The next year, he won his fifth batting title (.335), but with yet another team, the Brooklyn Superba. In 1894, he hit .347 and drove in 128 runs, leading Baltimore to its first pennant. In 1904, now at the age of 46, and in the minors, he won the Class D Hudson River League batting title. He ended the year with a two-game return to the Giants. Brouthers ended his career with a .343 batting average, the ninth-best of all time. He retired and worked as a press box attendant at the Polo Grounds until his death in 1932. He was elected to the Hall of Fame in 1945.

"Dear Old Roger" Connor (1857–1931) was the Babe Ruth of the nineteenth century, and his 138 homers were tops until the real Babe broke the record. He led the league in home runs in 1890, RBIs in 1889, and batting average in 1885. At 6 foot, 2 inches and 185 pounds, he joined the Troy Trojans in 1880. As the story goes, he found both his career and his wife in Troy when he went to a shirt factory where she worked; he had to be fitted with a special uniform because of his size and she took his measurements. He led the league in fielding average in 1887, 1890, 1892, and 1896. He is fifth on the all-time list of triples, with 233. On September 10, 1881, Connor was the first player to hit a grand slam in the major leagues.

In his debut season for New York Gothams (Giants), Connor batted .357. He hit such a homer in his first game with the Giants, in 1883, that fans passed the hat and bought him a $500 gold watch in appreciation. In 1885, Connor led the National League with 169 hits, batting .371. The following year, he led the league in triples and batted .355. In 1887, he smacked 17 home runs. In his teams first pennant win in 1888, Connor smacked 14 home runs; the next year, and another pennant, he hit 13 homers. In 18 seasons, he held a .317 batting average and was voted into the Hall of Fame in 1976.

William "Buck" Ewing (1859–1906) played several positions but was hailed as the best catcher in baseball during his time. Ewing batted a lifetime .303 but hit as high as .344 in 1893. During the infamous Dead Ball era, he was the National League home run champ, hitting 10 in 1883, and led the league with 83. Leading the league with 20 triples in 1884, he hit three of them in one game, and four other times, he hit 15 in a season. Ewing was fast too. He averaged 37 stolen bases and had a high of 53 in 1888.

Ewing also managed the New York, Cincinnati, and Cleveland clubs. In 1888, as manager, he led the Giants to their first pennant and did it again the next year, while also hitting .327. He was inducted into the Hall of Fame the year it opened, 1939.

"Sir Timothy" Keefe (1857–1933) joined the Troy team in 1880 and ended up playing for the New York Mets and Giants after the team quit the National League in 1882. Keefe

William "Buck" Ewing is pictured here with team mascot in 1887. Ewing batted .303 lifetime but hit as high as .344 in 1893.

is known as the inventor of the changeup and led the league in wins in 1888 and E.R.A. in 1880, 1885, and 1888. Keefe won 342 games during his career, which included winning 19 games in a row. He threw a six-or-less hitter 28 times in 51 starts in 1888 and went 4-0 in the World Series. His career E.R.A. was a low 2.62, and his record low of 0.80 pitched in 1880 remains a record today. Keefe ended his baseball career as an umpire but made his money in real estate. He was elected to the Hall of Fame in 1964.

"Smiling Mickey" Welch (1859–1941) was a right-handed pitcher with a curveball, a change of pace, and a screwball and was the third 300-game winner of the majors. He threw seven 20-plus games in a row and nine total in his 13-year stint. He joined Troy in 1880.

During his 13 Major League seasons, he posted 20 or more wins nine times—seven in succession. In 1884, he completed 62 of 65 starts, winning 39, and had a career-high 345 strikeouts. He established a record by striking out the first nine batters he faced, a feat that was not broken until 1970. Welch won 17 consecutive games in 1885, with 7 of them shutouts, and won 44 games, losing only 11. He lead the National League with an .800 winning percentage and also logged 40 career shutouts. On September 10, 1889, he made history by becoming the first pinch-hitter in Major League history. Welch helped pitch the Giants to their first pennant. He remains among the leaders in complete games and innings pitched. Welch was elected to the Hall of Fame in 1973.

Michael "King" Kelly, a Troy native, was considered one of the greatest players of his time. He has been called the King of Baseball, but his $10,000 salary was considered exorbitant by some.

Two other Trojans are in the Hall of Fame, although they never played with the Troy team. Troy-born John "The Trojan" Evers was the pivot man in baseball's most famous double-play combination, "Tinker to Evers to Chance." He helped lead Chicago to four National League pennants and two World Championships (1907, 1908). Evers led the Boston Braves to a World Series title in 1914, batting .438 in the series, and was voted the Most Valuable Player. He was elected to the Hall of Fame in 1946. Evers is the only Hall of Famer buried locally in St. Mary's in Troy.

Trojan Michael "King" Kelly began his professional baseball career with Cincinnati and is considered one of the greatest players of his time. He stole at least 50 bases in four consecutive years, including 84 in 1887, and played on 8 pennant winners in 16 years. He won the National League batting title in 1884 (.354) and 1886 (.388). He was elected to the Hall of Fame in 1945.

Trojans contributed to the great game of baseball in other ways, too. Third baseman Esteban Enrique Bellan, otherwise known as Steve "the Cuban Sylph," was the first Latin player in professional baseball. More than 50 years before Jackie Robinson broke the color barrier, Troy's Haymakers employed a Latino player, born in Havana, Cuba, in a league that otherwise was pure white. Bellan is credited as being the father of baseball in Cuba. Alec Smith of Troy made the first catcher's mitt in the 1880s. Troy's James N. Kern became the first president of the National Association League when it formed in 1876.

BROADWAY ON THE HUDSON

Troy had several burlesque and vaudeville houses as it moved into the twentieth century, and of course, several movie houses when the talkies became popular. Troy was no stranger to producing original music either in the vein of grand marches, waltzes, or rag time. The city even inspired a hit Broadway musical.

The year 1923 was particularly interesting. It is the year that the first wireless telephone call was made from New York to London. Jack Dempsey defended his heavyweight boxing title against Luis Firpo. Yankee Stadium opened in New York City and Rin Tin Tin made his film debut. More plays were produced on Broadway in the 1920s than in any other period, and in 1923, the city of Troy was featured in a hit musical called *Helen of Troy, New York.*

Helen of Troy, New York was written by the legendary George S. Kaufman (1889–1961) and Marc Connelly (1890–1980) from their book of the same name. The musical numbers were written by Bert Kalmar and Harry Ruby with titles like "Look for the Happy Ending," "It Was Meant to Be," "Cry Baby," "Keep a Goin' " (the show's hit song), "The Small Town Girl," "I Like a Big Town," "I Like a Small Town," "What Makes a Business Man Tired," "What the Girls Will Wear," "My Ideal," "Nijigo Novgo," and "Helen of Troy, New York."

Kaufman, who was a playwright and journalist, was the most successful writer in American theater between World Wars I and II. He won the Pulitzer Prize twice for plays of which he was coauthor. He wrote some 40 plays, and half were hits. He was the drama critic for the *New York Times* from 1917 to 1930.

His first successful play *Dulcy*, starring Lynn Fontanne, was written in collaboration with Marc Connelly and first performed in 1921. Two years later, they wrote the two-act *Helen of Troy, New York*, starring Helen Ford. While the play was more a financial failure than success due to its expensive set and large cast, it ran a solid 181 performances.

Connelly was also a playwright and journalist covering the theater for the *Morning Telegraph*. He is famous for his Pulitzer Prize–winning *Green Pastures*, a story of the Old Testament told through the lives of Southern blacks, but he is especially known for the comedies that he co-wrote with Kaufman. Kaufman and Connelly's *Dulcy* was followed by *To the Ladies* (1922), with Helen Hayes, and then *Helen of Troy, New York.*

The musical *Helen of Troy, New York* opened on Broadway on Tuesday, June 19, 1923, at the Selwyn Theater on Forty-second Street at 8:30 p.m. The play was introduced by Rufus LeMaire and George Jessel. It moved to the Times Square Theater and then hit the road in Boston, Allentown, and elsewhere.

Though some reviewers were not crazy about the score (one did call it "competent and catchy music"), Kaufman and Connelly received raves. The *Herald* said it was "the perfect musical comedy." *Tribune* critic Percy Hammond wrote, "It seems improbable that I shall ever again be asked if there exists in New York any musical plays in which bare legs and barer jokes do not abound."

Getting the play produced took some doing, and it wasn't their play originally. Kaufman and Connelly were approached by Rufus LeMaire, who had produced one previous hit, *Broadway Brevities*. The pair were not crazy about the play's title either, *Helen of Troy, New*

York, which they thought silly, but agreed nevertheless to write the book and the play. They found out soon after that financing for the play was coming from bootleggers, including the famous gambler Nick the Greek. When Nick went broke and the bootleggers' shipments were seized, LeMaire approached his friend and up-and-coming star George Jessel to invest. He did, to the tune of $10,000, his total savings. Jessel didn't recoup his money, although Kaufman and Connelly did. LeMaire sold his share after opening, moved to California, and became an executive at Universal.

Helen of Troy, New York was based on the story of working girls in the collar industry of Troy and pokes fun at the new corporate culture that was taking hold in America. This was modeled on the very successful advertising campaign of Cluett, Peabody that ran from 1905 to 1931. The collar company's ad campaign appeared nationally and, in particular, in the *Saturday Evening Post*, an upscale magazine.

The Cluett company contracted with artist Joseph C. Leyendecker to develop a winning look for their Arrow collars. The result was the first successful introduction of sex as a selling tool; all of his beautifully illustrated ads displayed male and female models responding to the sex appeal of the "Arrow Man." During this time, most men in the country were wearing collars from Troy, but made by a number of collar companies.

Pulitzer Prize–winning writer George F. Kaufman and Marc Connelly penned the successful Broadway play based on Troy female collar workers in 1923.

Cluett cashed in by creating the "Arrow Man" and captured most of the market. This was the predecessor of the now familiar "Marlboro Man" and other brand "models" that followed. *Helen of Troy, New York* seems to be a response to this, and besides lampooning mass advertising, the play was rather eccentric and even had a weird number with Russian folk dancers and an instrumental number with ukuleles and other strange instruments.

One writer wasn't surprised at the eccentricity, considering that Kaufman eventually wrote three Marx Brothers movies, *The Cocoanuts* (1929), *Animal Crackers* (1930), and *A Night at the Opera* (1935), while his buddies Kalmar and Ruby wrote the songs for *Animal Crackers*. Kalmar and Ruby also wrote *Horse Feathers* (1932) and *Duck Soup* (1933) in addition to the music.

HOLLYWOOD ON THE HUDSON

Two years after the debut of *Helen of Troy* during the rag time era, a baby girl was born to a woman who worked for the Labor Department in Troy. This baby grew up to be a star of the stage, screen, and later television. Local folks like to point out that the Capital District area was the home of several stars of the stage and screen during the golden years, like Kirk Douglas and Bill Devane. But there are two ladies that Troy is famous for: Helen, of course, and Maureen Stapleton, a living legend.

Maureen Stapleton is all Troy! Born in 1925, she grew up on First Street. The versatile star is one of the few actresses that have crossed over to all media, being successful in film, theater, and television. Her first major stage success was in *The Rose Tattoo* (1951), and she is best known for playing intelligent character roles. Her first appearance on Broadway was in *Orpheus Descending* (1957), then *Toys in the Attic* (1960), *The Gingerbread Lady* (1970), and *The Country Girl* (1973). Her films include *A View from the Bridge* (1962), *Plaza Suite* (1972), *Reds* (1981), *Cocoon* (1985), and *Nuts* (1988). She even did the voice in *Snow Cat*, a 1998 animated short film.

Stapleton won the Academy Award for supporting actress for her performance in *Reds* in 1981. As one reviewer said, "She has received the highest acclaim for her great emotional power and versatility." She is a charter member of the renowned Actors Studio and has won the top honors granted to performing artists, including the Oscar, Emmy, and Tony Awards. Few actors have been so successful in all media. In 1995, she and Jane Scoville wrote her autobiography called *A Hell of a Life*, full of great stories. Another book, *Maureen Stapleton: A Bio Bibliography* is the first book dedicated to the career of this consummate actress. In 1981, her Academy Award year, Hudson Valley Community College dedicated the Maureen Stapleton Theater with the actress there to help celebrate.

GOING TO THE THEATERS

Going to the movies was a common and popular event and one that took some thought not too long ago. There were a dozen movie houses in the city. Old timers will remember the Lincoln on Third Street or the American on River. The Palace sat on Fifth Avenue and Hoosick. The Rose, later called State, was on Fourth by Congress. The Arlington was on Pawling Avenue. The Bijou and Lansing entertained in Lansingburgh. The Griswold and

Proctor's Theatre, on the east side of Fourth Street, was built in 1913–1914 as a vaudeville house. It was closed in 1978 but still stands.

Shea's Five Cent Theater were on Third. The Rivoli was on Second. Lastly, the Troy on River and Proctor's on Fourth were the city's premier movie stops. Many of these theaters offered the finest Hollywood productions until the 1970s, and tickets cost no more than 10¢ to 50¢ for a movie. Many remember standing in the ticket line that went around the block—twice—at Proctor's on Fourth Street.

Today's generation can thank Thomas Edison, Louis Lumiere, Bell Labs, and others for the technology that makes movie magic. During the early twentieth century, short silent films, or "flickers," were offered in vaudeville houses, often as the last item of the night or between performances. The Griswold Theater was leased to Frederick F. Proctor in 1905 and remodeled as Proctor's Griswold Theater.

In their heyday, the movies were a way for common folk to escape the drudgery of work and feel like royalty while doing it. Hollywood wanted everyone to feel special, and they did whatever it took to make people feel that way. The largest picture palaces, like the San Francisco Fox and the Roxy, had a full-staffed hospital in case of emergencies. The Roxy's hospital staff (physicians, surgeons, and nurses) treated more than 12,000 patients in its male and female wards during the first year it was opened. Nurseries were available in most palaces; and in some, like the Loew's Seventy-second Street in New York City, they took care of pets while the owners enjoyed the show.

Even the bathrooms were richly decorated, including being staffed by attendants. When the famous Vanderbilt family demolished their Manhattan townhouse in the mid-1920s, Loew's bought much of the interior and had its workers dismantle their "Oriental Room" and bring it in pieces to Kansas City. It became the Women's Lounge of the Loew's Midland Theater in 1927.

No, Troy's Proctor's Theater was not that elaborate, but still, there are many Trojans who can tell of their first movie experience at Proctor's. Proctor's was one of those places in Troy that didn't care to what social class one belonged—the movies were open to everyone.

Proctor's "New Theater" on Fourth, which he promoted as having "Super Vaudeville" and "Supreme Photo-Plays," was built in 1913–1914 and billed as "Troy's Largest Amusement Place." One of the earliest shows, premiering on February 2, 1914, was a Warner's feature movie, *The Mothers Penitent*, a drama of the golden West starring Baby Early and Elsie Albert. In 1917, Fred and Adele Astaire (before Ginger) appeared in person to "new songs and distinctive dance."

The first real success in synchronizing sound and film was achieved in 1922 by Bell Telephone Laboratories with their creation of the Vitaphone. Samuel L. Warner, of Warner Brothers, was so impressed by it that he committed the studio to develop motion pictures with sound. He created the Vitaphone Corporation in April 1926, with exclusive license to utilize the new technology. Only four months later, Warner released the first Vitaphone feature production, *Don Juan*. The movie was filmed as a silent, but given a synchronized musical score. Along with the film were several Vitaphone-produced shorts, including a talkie and some songs to show off the new technology. There were only 12 movie theaters in the country and not much of a viewing public, but nonetheless, it was a hit.

William Fox, president of the Fox Film Corporation, saw the potential of Warner's efforts and purchased the competing Case-Sponable system for recording and synchronizing sound on film, which he renamed Movietone. In the spring of 1927, Fox released a Movietone that featured sound shorts of the outdoors, something not possible with Vitaphone technology. Audiences were delighted to the sights and sounds of the morning drills of West Point cadets and Charles Lindbergh's transatlantic takeoff.

Not to be outdone, Warner released *The Jazz Singer*, with Al Jolson, on October 23, 1927, complete with the very first dialogue ever recorded for a feature. It premiered in New York City at Warner's Strand. The following year, the Troy Theater, built only four years previous as a "silent," was billing itself as the "House of the Talkies."

Vaudeville and movies often shared the same stage. On November 9, 1929, one could see both Ruth Chatterton in *Once a Lady* and Rose's Midgets on the same bill at Proctor's. Rose's "25 Lilliputians" were billed as "the Largest Company of Midgets in the World with the Only Midget Jazz Band." Quite a show, no doubt.

By 1931, there were 11 theaters in the Troy area, offering such entertainment as Joan Crawford in *This Modern Age*, Buster Keaton in *Sidewalks of New York*, Eddie Cantor in *Palmy Days*, and the double feature at the Palace of Maurice Chevalier's *The Smiling Lieutenant* and Bert Wheeler's *Caught Plastered*.

The next 30 years were the golden age for movie theaters. At the State Theater during the 1960s, admission was a dime (two features and a cartoon). So was popcorn, and

Goldberg's Peanut Chews only cost a nickel. Often, a serial featuring Batman or Flash Gordon played between features. Bingo was offered after the show.

With the 1950s came the proliferation of television sets. The movie studios countered with 3-D, Cinemascope, and VistaVision as an attempt to lure viewers back. Moveover, it was the time of drive-in movies and grade B science-fiction films that featured aliens (substitutes for the Communist threat) with their zippered suits and flying saucers on strings.

By the early 1970s, suburban expansion and, later, Troy's reckless urban removal period rang the death knell. One had to get in the car and leave the city to see a movie. Proctor's continued to provide entertainment until the day it closed in the 1970s. Unfortunately, it has been vacant and deteriorating for more than 20 plus now and has become a shelter for pigeons and the homeless. The American Theater became "specialized" and is the sole remaining "movie" house in Troy. An attempt to bring first-rate movies to town occurred with the building of the Atrium, but it suffered the same fate.

TROY'S ROLLER COASTER DAYS

On the east side of Fifth Avenue, between 108th and 110th Streets, and running east to the foot of Oakwood Cemetery, is a tranquil, nicely kept residential area of Lansingburgh. But on this same spot 80 years ago, one would have heard the cries of Midway barkers, the thunder of running horses, the laughter of children, and the roar of a roller coaster. This 42-acre parcel of land was one of the finest amusement parks in the country and was known as Rensselaer Park. Its tag line was "The Real Pleasure Ground for the Pleasure Bound."

Rensselaer Park had a half-mile racetrack and Midway amusement area tucked away within a huge, beautiful grove of trees. Today, it survives only in memories and a few photographs. The entrance to Rensselaer Park was on Fifth Avenue just north of 108th Street (108th Street did not extend east of Fifth). The park was organized in 1867 as the Rensselaer Park Association, but originally served as a training ground for Union soldiers and was called Camp Willard during the Civil War. An army hospital was also established there. The buildings were used as a hospital for a cholera epidemic and later as a slaughterhouse complex. The building also housed the Rensselaer County Fair for years. The park closed in 1917 and the land was sold in 1919, eventually being turned into the residential neighborhood located there now.

One of the big draws of the park was the carousel, called the Menagerie. For a quarter, one could ride hand-carved horses, bears, giraffes, camels, lions, elephants, and goats. After the park closed, the carousel ended up in Halfmoon Beach, a few miles east of Troy. Eventually, the carousel was sold along with the individual animals.

Among the many other amusements was a small 10-seat Ferris wheel. The world's first Ferris wheel, at 264 feet high, debuted at the 1893 World's Colombian Exposition and was invented by RPI graduate George Ferris. The Exposition also had the first Midway, called the Midway Plaisance (or White City Midway). Its well-lit, fancy building facades dictated how amusement parks would be designed for the following 60 years.

It was difficult to get bored at Rensselaer Park. There was a bowling alley, a high-wire act, pony rides, a figure-eight wooden roller coaster, a dancing pavilion, a skating rink, and a band shell where concerts were held every afternoon and evening. Fireworks were held every Thursday night.

For only a dime, one could view Bama the Ostrich Girl, step up to the Hindu Theater, watch wild animals get tamed, or be in awe as a man or J.W. Groman's High Diving Horses leaped from a tower into a lake that was located within the southern portion of the racetrack. The 1.5-mile racetrack, fully visible in all directions, filled the eastern part of the park in sharp contrast to the densely wooded Midway section. People lined up on the northern part of the track, complete with a grandstand and judges tower, to watch harness, bicycle, and even chariot races. The park had its own police squad to direct traffic and handle the mobs of people that frequented the park.

The Haymakers, the local baseball team that became the foundation for the New York Giants, played here during the park's first year. In 1868, the same year the racetrack, the secondary road around it, and the pond were built, the team drew from 5,000 to 9,000 people to one game. The park trustees built them a U-shaped bleacher somewhere near the track.

Rensselaer Park in Lansingburgh was where many a Trojan enjoyed harness racing, roller coasters, and other amusement rides during the early twentieth century. The park closed after World War I.

Eliza Waters's son created the first paper boat, and this father-and-son business soon went on to make observatory domes, cartridge boxes for the Union army, saddle trees, and many other paper products.

One strange incident occurred at the park and was reported in the papers. A cannibal with one of the shows bit a Lansingburgh resident, and the local newspapers proclaimed that the man would probably die as a result of the bite. The cannibal escaped, but no information regarding the victim has been uncovered to date.

While amusement parks got their start in the United States in the nineteenth century, they date back to medieval Europe and were known then as pleasure gardens. Areas were set aside and created specifically for outdoor entertainment and amusement. These first parks included fountains and flower gardens, but also included games, bowling, music, dancing, shows, and a few primitive amusement rides. In 1583, an amusement park opened in Bakken, north of Copenhagen. It is still in operation today. By 1919, at the end of Rensselaer Park's life, there were over 1,500 amusement parks still in operation in the United States. By 1935, after the stock market crash, the number dwindled to only 400.

TROY'S PAPER BOATS

Paper is truly a remarkable invention! As early as 4,000 B.C., ancient Egyptians used papyrus, a type of paper made from a woven mat of reeds and pounded into a hard, thin sheet. Ancient Greeks used parchment that was made from animal skins. But paper as we know it today was invented in China in 105 A.D. Historical records show that its invention was reported that year to the Chinese emperor by Ts'ai Lun, an official of the

Imperial Court. Although recent archeology has pushed the date back 200 years, the fact remains that paper has been around for a very long time.

While we all use paper for communication (and occasionally making paper airplanes), there were many other uses put to the product when it was first introduced into America in the eighteenth century. Paper has been used for making clothes, train car wheels, observatory domes, coffins, and even boats! Yes, boats, and that of course brings us to Troy.

Eliza Waters, formerly a druggist, and his son opened a factory at 303 River Street and began making paper boxes. According to historians, that all changed when George Waters, the teen-aged son of Eliza, was invited to a masquerade party in 1867. Instead of paying $8 for a mask, he borrowed a mask and made a paper replica of it using paper and paste from his father's factory.

Impressed with his success, he attempted to fix a leaky cedar rowing shell that he picked up by varnishing and gluing paper to portions of the hull. It was this success that led George and his father, in June of that year, to build the world's first paper boat. By using the hull of a wooden rowing shell as the mold, they glued stripes of paper in unbroken lengths from stem to stern and varnished them together. This first paper boat was christened *The Experiment*.

Only one year after the first Waters' paper boat was constructed, in 1868, paper racing hulls won 14 water races, followed by 26 wins the following year, making quite a splash with the rowing public. In 1871, the Waters issued a 400-plus-page *Catalogue and Oarsman's Manual*. By 1875, the pair were producing more than 45 different racing shells, row boats, and canoes, and the *New York Daily Graphic* declared that they had the largest boat factory in the United States. That same year, a Cornell crew rowing a paper six-oared boat, beat 10 other colleges in wooden boats at Saratoga Lake, and the following year, paper boats swept all events in the Centennial Regatta.

Waters' paper boats were not only used for racing. Pleasure canoes were also made, and two people helped make the Waters name famous. Reporter Julius J. Chambers planned a trip from the headwaters of the Mississippi to its mouth in New Orleans. In May 1872, he began his voyage at the White Earth Indian Reservation in central Minnesota with his paper boat. A month later, he made it to Lake Itasca and explored the tributaries feeding the lake but terminated his trip just short of his final destination. He penned reports of the trip in the *New York Herald*.

Another adventurer, Nathaniel Holmes Bishop, began a trip from Quebec to the Gulf Coast of Florida in 1874 using a conventional wooden canoe. When he reached Troy in his wooden canoe, he discovered the Waters' paper boat factory, ordered one, and abandoned his wooden one—and his assistant. Liberated from both, he eventually made it south. He wrote a popular book of his exploits called the *Voyage of the Paper Canoe*, detailing his trip and his paper boat, and it was quite a hit with the public.

Fast and light, Waters' paper boats became dominant for 30 years. However, the Waters family didn't rest on their laurels. In 1878, they built a paper observatory dome 29 feet in diameter for the newly erected Proudfit Observatory at RPI. Using the same construction techniques that were used to make their boats, thick linen paper was placed over dome molds. The 16 individually cast sections were then bolted together forming the 2-ton observatory dome. It was removed 20 years later when the building was remodeled in 1889. They continued making domes around the country, including one 30 feet in diameter for the U.S. Academy at West Point.

The paper boat industry literally was born and died with its founders. Shortly after George accidentally burned the factory down in 1901, George and Eliza died in 1902 and 1904, respectively. Only three Waters' paper boats are known to survive today; one is currently on display at the Burden Iron Museum in Troy. The paper boat industry was a short-lived industry, but it is another example of the entrepreneurial spirit that was so pervasive during Troy's industrial heyday.

The Troy Boys Club was created in 1899 by Frank G. Simmons to provide aid to poor boys. The group's first home was in the Boardman building, and in 1904, Harvey S. McLeod, vice president of Union Bank, remodeled and refitted the upper two floors of 311 River Street, seen here in 1906. When this picture was taken, the club had 857 boys. The Boys Club still serves Troy's youth—both boys and girls—as the Troy Boys and Girls Club.

14. Natural Disasters

There is an old saying about not being able to fool Mother Nature. Before the days of Doppler radar and sophisticated firefighting technology, many old cities had to deal with nature's wrath the best way possible. Lightning starts a forest fire every 3 seconds somewhere in the world. Most natural habitats are shaped by fire, and even some, like pine barrens, require fire to maintain the species diversity that has evolved there. It just so happens that fire has also been an integral part of the evolution of most major nineteenth-century cities in the country, and Troy is no exception.

Troy had several fires in 1803, 1820, 1848, 1854, and 1862 that had major loss of buildings but, fortunately, little loss of life. The first fire began on May 1, 1803, at the hat shop of Jonathan Hatch on River Street and spread to the entire block of buildings between Fulton and Grand Division Streets. On June 20, 1820, a fire began in the stable behind the home of Colonel Thomas Davis on (35) First Street in Troy. Before it was over, some 90 buildings (69 stores and dwellings) in the business section of Troy, stretching from the west side of First Street between Congress and Broadway and encompassing all of that part of State Street, down to River Street down to the river banks, were destroyed. This fire destroyed about one-ninth of the total number of buildings in the city at that time.

Many people, including wealthy merchants, were in need of help, and between the citizens of Troy and folks as far away as New York City, more than $14,000 was raised, along with donations of clothing, furniture, and food. The total loss of property was estimated at $700,000. Shocked by the severity of the fire, the following month, on July 8, the city council passed an ordinance stating, "No person shall smoke or carry any lighted or burning segar or pipe, in any street, alley, barn, stable, or outhouse in the city, upon pain of forfeiting and paying for each and every such offence, the penalty of one dollar." Yet, a smaller fire on September 5, 1827, in the same area destroyed a number of buildings on the east side of River Street.

The year 1848 was also not a good one for the city. On May 1, around 9:30 a.m., fire broke out in the stable at the rear of Halsted's Merchant Hall. The Mechanics Hall and all but two other buildings on the east side of River Street between Congress and Ferry Streets were burned.

On Friday afternoon, August 25, 1854, a steam planing mill on the southwest corner of Front and Division Streets caught on fire. More than seven blocks of buildings burned,

This scene, looking southwest from the intersection of Fulton and Union Streets, was photographed after the 1862 fire. Troy University, at top, was unharmed.

including nine lumberyards and many businesses, mostly on First, River, and Front Streets between Jefferson and Division. Two hundred buildings were lost, leaving 300 families homeless. More than $1 million worth of damage occurred.

No one could have foreseen the next disaster. On the afternoon of May 10, 1862, sparks from a locomotive sitting on the wooden bridge of the Rensselaer & Saratoga Railroad (now the site of the Green Island Bridge) ignited the wooden structure. Before it was over, more than 500 buildings including homes, mansions, churches, public buildings, colleges, banks, and the Union Station, covering 75 acres of downtown Troy, were gone. The center of the city was a pile of ash. Remarkably, only five people, including one child, were killed.

By July, two months after the fire, 181 new buildings had been erected or restored. By November, six months after the fire that burned most of downtown Troy, all building lots except for two were occupied by new or rebuilt structures. Remarkably, a year after the fire, on May 9, 1863, a covered pile of coal was found still smoldering in the cellar of a business at 376 River Street.

Even downtown Lansingburgh didn't escape the ravages of fire. On Sunday, July 9, 1843, around 40 buildings between Second and Third Avenues and 116th to 118th Streets burned to the ground. Two weeks later, more buildings burned on Second Avenue between 116th and 117th Streets. Those homes and businesses were rebuilt.

In the 14-year period between 1848 and 1862, more than 1,000 homes and businesses burned to the ground, covering most of the Troy area. For the period after the great fire of 1862 and up to 1925, Troy experienced close to 70 more fires, in which a two alarm or more was called. These usually consisted of large mills or factory buildings, theaters, stores, or other large structures.

SLIDING INTO HISTORY

In the early summer of 1836, a large part of the western slope of Mount Ida separated from itself and slid to the base. No one was hurt in that first recorded landslide in Troy. However, the following year, on Sunday evening, January 1, 1837, another large part of the mount near Washington Street slid at least 500 feet from the base, destroying 3 homes, killing 7 people, and sweeping away 2 stables with 16 horses.

History repeated itself a few years later. On November 14, 1840, on a Saturday evening, and the following Monday, two more landslides made their way down, crushing one house but fortunately not hurting anyone. Two years after that, on a Friday afternoon, another slide near Washington killed 15 people and demolished 10 structures, marking the most disastrous slide Troy has ever experienced. Finally, on the evening of March 17, 1859, Washington Street was hit again; the landslide wiped out the unfinished building of St. Peter's College. As a reminder of those geological principles described here, the last major slip of Mount Ida can be seen by drivers traveling along Interstate 787 on the west bank of the Hudson River.

The Trojan Hook and Ladder Company heads south on Third Street across from City Hall.

There have been no major slips of Mount Ida since 1859. Throughout the nineteenth century, many homes were built along Ferry Street up the hill and along the northern base of the mount with no problems. Unfortunately, they were destroyed not by landslide, but by urban renewal and the ill-fated original Interstate 787 plan during the 1970s, which had the road going through Troy instead of its present route through Watervliet.

WATER AND SNOW

If fire and landslides were not enough, developing a city along the banks of a major river valley also has its problems—floods. Being only a few feet above sea level, Troy has had a series of major floods. The most notable took place in March 1647 when two whales found their way to Troy due to high water and one became stranded on an island (now submerged by the State Dam). The whale became beached, and enterprising Trojans extracted as much whale oil as they could. The whole region smelled for weeks due to the rotting carcass, and oil was found on the surface of the river nearby for three weeks.

On March 2, 1818, one-fourth of the city was covered by water 18 inches above the norm. Topping that was the flood in March 12, 1832, which was 18 inches higher than the previous one and made its way up to Fifth Avenue as far north as Congress. A flood in 1857 ripped off a railroad bridge above the State Dam and tossed it against the north side of the covered bridge of the Rensselaer & Saratoga Railroad. In February 1886, the section of Troy from River, First, Second, Third, north to Liberty and Fourth, Fifth Avenue, and beyond Ferry Street were inundated.

The Hudson rose 28 feet and flooded the River Street collar district on March 28, 1913.

More than 4 feet of snow fell on Troy on March 13, 1888.

On March 28, 1913, however, no one could brace for the flood that rose 2.5 feet above the flood of 1886—totalling 28 feet above sea level. This flood covered everything, including Washington Park, Ferry Street, Fifth Avenue, First Street, Liberty Street and Square, Second, Third, Fourth, and Congress Streets, Van Buren Street, and, for the first time ever, Franklin Square. This was repeated in 1936, and even though flood control programs have been put into effect since, Troy continues to have floods that rise close to present-day River Street.

Water takes other forms! In 1888, more than 4 feet of snow fell on the area, creating the infamous blizzard of '88 and bringing the city to a standstill.

Troy experienced a variety of other odd-ball weather conditions throughout its history. In 1816, Troy, or for that matter, much of the Northeast, did not have a summer season. In May, there was a half-inch of ice that killed much of the vegetation. On June 8, there was ice and up to 3 inches of snow falling in Troy. On July 5, there was a coating of ice that was the thickness of windowpane glass. It was known as the "year without a summer." It also had two other names: "poverty year" and "eighteen hundred froze to death."

This is what *Harper's Bazaar* reported for the year 1816:

Both January and February of 1816 were warm and springlike, so much so that settlers let their fireplaces die. The cold started in March, with each day windy and blustery. Despite the weather, spring crops were planted, with vegetation well under way by April when unusual cold moved in. Snow or sleet fell for 17 different days in May, killing the fruit trees. June saw frost and snow for all but 3 days, it lasted through July. August was worse, with ice coating the fields, vegetation was gone, wildlife had moved to distant lands and panic felled upon the people.

What was the cause of this anomaly? Three major volcanic eruptions took place between 1812 and 1817. Volcano Soufriere on St. Vincent Island erupted in 1812, followed by Mayon in the Philippines in 1814, and Tamboro on the island of Sumbawa in Indonesia in 1815. Tambora had the most dramatic effect. This 13,000-foot volcano blew flame and ash from April 7 to 12, 1815, and blew from 37 to 100 cubic miles of dust, ash, and cinders into the atmosphere, generating a globe-girdling veil of volcanic dust.

On January 4, 1835, Troy experienced one of its coldest days ever. It was 32 degrees below zero at sunrise. A month later, the eruption of Nicaragua's Mount Coseguina in February 1835 cooled the world with the effects of its dustveil. Historical climatologists regard 1835 and 1836 as particularly cool years.

On September 6, 1881, the Northeast and Troy experienced a day that appeared to have no daylight. The sky was dark all day, with a yellow and brassy appearance and virtually no sunlight. This may have been the result of a major set of fires in Michigan, in which 20 villages burned as forest fires raged on that day. The smoke filtered out most of the light and left a brassy tinge on everything downwind for hundreds of miles. Some 500 people were killed in the fires.

Trojans were also rocked by two minor earthquakes. The first occurred on Sunday, August 10, 1884, at 2:07 p.m. and moved from north to south. The second struck on Sunday, November 4, 1877, at 1:53 a.m. No injuries were reported.

The city of Troy certainly had its share of natural and manmade disasters, but the city, named after the fabled Troy that had seven lives, survived and lived up to its name.

Accidents were not uncommon among Troy's steamers, trains, and trolleys.

15. TROY'S THIRD CENTURY

Troy entered the twentieth century in a strong social and economic condition. The city annexed one-time rival Lansingburgh in 1900, adding another 10,000 people to the 60,651 inhabitants of the city, thereby raising its ranking to 62 in the top 100 U.S. cities in terms of population. Troy continued to grow during the early part of the twentieth century and reached its highest population recorded by the U.S. census in 1910, with 76,813 (ranked 72, at the time). The 1920 census figure of 72,013 was disputed, and a local count produced 81,014 (37,211 male, 43,803 female) residents.

The 1920 census revealed that there were 8 percent more women in Troy than men. This is not surprising since the collar and cuff industry was the number-one industry in the city, employing 9,932 people, with 7,565 of them women. Next to collars and cuffs, the Troy Chamber of Commerce ranked foundry and machine shops, brushes, clothing, printing, publishing, and paper box making as the six most important industries at the time.

The iron industry was still strong. Horseshoe output was at 12 million sets a year. Troy bells were still being made and ringing worldwide. The largest valves in the world were constructed here by both Ludlow and Ross Valve. Stewart-brand (Fuller & Warren) cast-iron stoves were still heating millions of homes around the world. Large land projects were surveyed with Gurley's scientific instruments, made in Troy. The city was second in the country in production of brushes, and more than 268 incorporated companies in the city were producing hundreds of products. More than 34,000 wage earners, almost half the population, were working in a Troy industry.

In 1916, a harbor and dock commission began rebuilding the docks from the Barge Canal terminal at Adams to Broadway. These new concrete docks, a mile long and still in existence, were completed in 1924. The Barge Canal terminal from Washington to Adams Streets was fitted with cranes and hand derricks and a large grain elevator. Dredging of the river also occurred and allowed the steamers to dock at Broadway's steamboat landing once again. The Green Island bridge was raised 10 inches and a new drawbridge added to accompany the additional water traffic.

New housing developments began to take place in the eastern parts of the city along Hoosick, Sycaway, and Albia, replacing open fields. Things were looking so well that Troy's city engineer, Alfred E. Roche, eagerly predicted in 1916 the future of the new "Greater Troy" as follows:

I predict for the city of Troy a future in which we will see a revival of the great iron industry; that we will see those unoccupied stretches of land humming with industrial life; and that we will become one of the principal cities along the river and canals for receiving, storing and discharging the immense quantities of grain now floating to the western terminus of the canal. I predict that the industrial section along the riverfront with factories, foundries, storehouses, barge and freight line, steamboats, ocean trawlers, of twelve-foot draught, grain elevators served by water and rail, with equal facilities for interchange of business, will give abundant employment and stimulate Troy's commercial prosperity.

Trojans were optimistic about their future, but the powerhouse industrial days of the city were over. Population began to decline by 1930 to 72,763, and continued for the remainder of the century. In fact, Troy has steadily declined from a population high of 76,813 (1900 census) to 49,170 (2000 census), a drop of 27,740 people, a figure that closely matches Troy's 1875 population.

Pedestrians and an open-air trolley cross the market block, c. 1913.

Most of the buildings in this 1910 photo of Third Street are now gone. Frear's is on the immediate right.

The advent of suburbs and the flight of industry from the Northeast began to take a toll on Troy. Industries such as iron and steel moved west. The collar and cuff industry already replaced by shirt making moved south, although a few companies still stayed in Troy. With the coming of malls, faster automobiles, and the desire to get out of the "gritty" city away from noise, crime, and any other excuse one could imagine, Troy lost not only its manufacturing base, but its labor force as well.

By the 1950s, railroads were no longer stopping in Troy. In fact the ornate Union Depot was torn down in 1958 for a parking lot, a sign of things to come.

By the late 1960s and 1970s, the famous "urban renewal" period saw thousands of historic residential and commercial buildings wiped from the downtown landscape. This wholesale slaughter of the city's downtown was done in hopes that it would spur new commercial development so that Troy could compete with the malls and suburbia.

The devastated downtown area looked like a crater on the moon, as it sat, literally a hole for several years. Even today, the area has only a small motel and vacant restaurant (both with suburban design), and a parking garage to show for the massive demolition derby of several hundred buildings.

This view of Hoosick Street, looking east from River Street, was taken on April 11, 1908.

The same view as above but taken on August 20, 2001.

What is recognized today as the city's chief asset—historic architecture—was then a sign of a failing industrial economic base. Boarded-up buildings were a reminder of the former industrial heyday. Getting rid of them would make people forget, or so it seemed. The destruction of so many buildings also provided a reason not to go downtown. Historically, weekends saw so many shoppers on the streets, one would have to literally walk in the street to keep in motion. After the onslaught of urban removal, the city streets appeared as a ghost town. Those buildings not torn down were vacant and boarded up, and streets were pitted with pot holes.

Often the butt of jokes in the media, Troy went through political turmoil as one party tried to out-embarrass the other. The city became the regional mascot of urban decay and a symbol of the kind of place where no one wanted to live, let alone visit. Finally, in the late 1990s, near bankruptcy, the city even tried to mortgage City Hall. However, Troy is named for a city that rose from the ashes not once but seven times. New York's Troy has done the same.

The citizens of Troy elected members of the community that promised to clean things up fiscally as well as to restore the city's infrastructure. Troy's streets, sewers, and other infrastructure were repaired and old industrial buildings began to be renovated. What were once collar, cuff, and shirt manufacturing buildings now house New York State office workers.

Brick buildings that were once nineteenth-century retail stores now house computer software and other high-tech companies and are wired with twenty-first–century internet connections. Many of downtown's ornate office buildings are being renovated and reused as artist lofts or galleries. Historic residential row houses are being restored and lived in by new young (and old) professionals and families moving in from as far away as San Francisco.

Many are moving to Troy because of the beauty of the nineteenth-century streetscapes— the historic character and scale. Even Hollywood has discovered and used Troy as a backdrop for several movies, including *The Age of Innocence, Ironweed, The Bostonians, Scent of a Woman, Time Machine,* and *The Palace Thief.* To paraphrase a previous president—It's the history, stupid! Troy's past is the city's economic future.

Rensselaer Polytechnic Institute, the science school founded in a small Troy bank building some 175 years earlier, has developed a high-tech incubator program that keeps graduates in the area, discouraging their exodus to Boston or California's Silicon Valley. Today, there are over 100 software companies in the area.

It is estimated that by the year 2005 heritage tourism will be America's number-one industry. Already, Troy's visitor center, which promotes the history of the city, continues to attract more visitors each year. There are currently plans for a massive riverfront revitalization, which includes a bike trail from one end of Troy to the other. Unlike other cities along the Hudson River, Troy still has all of its original riverfront. Troy is undergoing a heritage renaissance.

Troy will never again become the industrial giant it once was, nor should it. The city, like any living organism, is undergoing evolution. While we may not exactly know the results of this evolution, one thing is certain: Troy has always been a city of experimentation. Very few cities have started so modestly and gone from such wealth to

The towers of Troy University, now replaced by RPI, stand watch over Mount Ida and the city in 1906.

Eighth Street appears in this view, looking north from Jacob Street. Eighth Street was virtually eliminated in the 1970s; there are very few homes remaining on this street.

such poverty and yet maintained such an optimistic vision for itself. Trojans will defend to the death their love for their city, and rightly so. With a history and tradition so rich, it is certain that the future of Troy will be filled with economic prosperity, a progressive citizenry, and continue to maintain a reputation for unwavering perseverance against all odds.

A parade goes by in this view looking south from Franklin Square, c. 1918. None of these buildings exist today; Harmony Hall is on the top left.

Bibliography

Dunn, Shirley W. *The Mohicans and Their Land, 1607–1730*. Fleischmanns, NY: Purple Mountain Press, 1994.

———. *The Mohican World, 1680–1750*. Fleischmanns, NY: Purple Mountain Press, 1994.

Hayner, Rutherford. *Troy and Rensselaer County, New York: A History*. New York: Lewis Historical Publishing Company, 1925.

Kalm, Peter. *Peter Kalm's Travels in North America: The English Version*. New York, Dover, 1966.

Ketchum, Alton. *Uncle Sam, the Man and the Legend*. New York: Hill and Wang, 1959.

Lansingburgh Bicentennial Committee. *Lansingburgh, New York: 200th Anniversary*. Troy: Lansingburgh Historical Society, 1971.

Rezneck, Samuel. *Profiles Out of the Past of Troy, New York, Since 1789*. Troy: Troy Chamber of Commerce, 1970.

Ritchie, William A. *Traces of Early Man in the Northeast*. Albany: New York State Museum & Science Service, 1957.

Rittner, Don. *Images of America: Troy*. Charleston, SC: Arcadia Publishing, 1998.

———. *Images of America: Lansingburgh*. Charleston, SC: Arcadia Publishing, 1999.

Sylvester, Nathaniel B. *History of Rensselaer County, New York*. Philadelphia: Everts and Peck, 1880.

Walkowitz, Daniel J. *Worker City, Company Town: Iron and Cotton-Worker Protests in Troy and Cohoes, New York, 1855–1884*. Urbana: University of Illinois Press, 1978.

Weise, Arthur J. *The City of Troy and Its Vicinity*. Troy: Edward Green, 1886.

———. *History of Lansingburgh, New York: From the Year 1670 to 1877*. Troy: William H. Young, 1877.

———. *Troy's One Hundred Years, 1789–1889*. N.p.: William H. Young, 1889.

Woodworth, John. *Reminiscences of Troy: From Its Settlement in 1790 to 1807*. Albany: Munsell, 1860.

This is a c. 1880 view of Troy, looking east on Federal Street from River Street. Most of what is visible here is now gone.

Index

This view, taken from Signal Tower #2 looking south toward Fulton Street, shows The Laurentian *ready to depart for New York City. The photograph was taken on March 12, 1955 by Jim Shaughnessy. Every building in this image is now gone.*

This view of the very busy Union Station and tracks, looking north from Signal Tower #1 at Broadway, was photographed in March 1955 by Jim Shaughnessy. Every building visible in this image is gone. The center tracks are now Sixth Avenue and the station area is occupied by the Raddock Building.

These contrasting views of the same intersection of Chatham and Franklin Squares show the destructive power of the 1970s urban renewal period. The scene above was captured c. 1890; the bottom in 2002.